Growing In Christ

Growing In Christ

Jim Cymbala

John Ortberg

Gary Thomas

Rick Warren

Mike Yaconelli

ZONDERVAN PUBLISHING COMPANY

www.zondervan.com

A Division of Harper Collins Publishers, Inc.

Published by Family Christian Stores, 5300 Patterson Avenue SE,
Grand Rapids, Michigan 49530.

ISBN 189306547-2

1 2 3 4 5 6 7 8 9 10

CONTENTS

Dear Valued Guest,

For more than seventy years, Family Christian Stores has had the privilege of impacting lives for Christ as a ministry-minded business. For this reason, we take extra care to offer one of the widest selections of Christian products designed to strengthen the hearts, minds and souls of believers and seekers from all ages and stages of life. This book you now hold in your hand is an extension of our mission. The Hearts, Minds & Souls series is an exclusive collection of books created to engage our guests in transforming and redemptive relationships with our Savior, Jesus Christ.

In addition to this book, the over ten thousand different products available in our stores and through FamilyChristian.com website provide a wealth of additional resources to address every need from a faith-filled, Christ-centered perspective. We have Bibles for everyone from young children just learning to read to seminary students serious about every nuance of Greek and Hebrew. We even have Bible accessories like covers, highlighters, tabs and more. We have books for men and women, singles and married couples, kids, tweens, teens and adults. We have music to minister to the hearts of every rhyme and rhythmical preference. From cards to tees, household items to framed art, pens to games, whatever your need, we promise you'll find something to enrich and enhance your lifestyle at Family Christian Stores.

We're also sensitive to your desire to be a good steward of the resources God has given you. That's why we offer a price matching promise, exclusive Perks program and great monthly deals on the latest most popular books and music. Flip to the back of this book, and you'll find valuable coupons to save even more money.

Thank you for shopping Family Christian Stores and FamilyChristian.com. We appreciate your partnership in reaching families and communities with the gospel and grace of Jesus Christ. We ask that you pray for us as we seek to operate our company in a way that best fulfills the mission God has given us.

Answering the call to help strengthen the hearts, minds & souls of our guests,

Dave Browne
President/CEO
Family Christian Stores

IT ALL STARTS WITH GOD

Rick Warren

For everything, absolutely everything, above and below, visible
and invisible,...everything got started in him and finds its purpose in him.
COLOSSIANS 1:16 (MSG)

Unless you assume a God, the question of life's purpose is meaningless.
BERTRAND RUSSELL, ATHEIST

It's not about you.

The purpose of your life is far greater than your own personal
fulfillment, your peace of mind, or even your happiness. It's far greater
than your family, your career, or even your wildest dreams and ambitions.
If you want to know why you were placed on this planet, you must
begin with God. You were born *by* his purpose and *for* his purpose.

The search for the purpose of life has puzzled people for thousands
of years. That's because we typically begin at the wrong starting point—
ourselves. We ask self-centered questions like What do *I* want to be?
What should *I* do with *my* life? What are *my* goals, *my* ambitions, *my*
dreams for *my* future? But focusing on ourselves will never reveal our
life's purpose. The Bible says, "It is God who directs the lives of his
creatures; everyone's life is in his power."[1]

Contrary to what many popular books, movies, and seminars tell
you, you won't discover your life's meaning by looking within yourself. You've probably tried that already. You didn't create yourself, so
there is no way you can tell yourself what you were created for! If I
handed you an invention you had never seen before, you wouldn't
know its purpose, and the invention itself wouldn't be able to tell you
either. Only the creator or the owner's manual
could reveal its purpose.

> *Focusing on ourselves
> will never reveal our
> life's purpose.*

I once got lost in the mountains. When I
stopped to ask for directions to the campsite,

I was told, "*You can't get there from here.* You must start from the other side of the mountain!" In the same way, you cannot arrive at your life's purpose by starting with a focus on yourself. You must begin with God, your Creator. You exist only because God wills that you exist. You were made *by* God and *for* God—and until you understand that, life will never make sense. It is only in God that we discover our origin, our identity, our meaning, our purpose, our significance, and our destiny. Every other path leads to a dead end.

Many people try to use God for their own self-actualization, but that is a reversal of nature and is doomed to failure. You were made for God, not vice versa, and life is about letting God use you for *his* purposes, not your using him for your own purpose. The Bible says, "Obsession with self in these matters is a dead end; attention to God leads us out into the open, into a spacious, free life."[2]

I have read many books that suggest ways to discover the purpose of my life. All of them could be classified as "self-help" books because they approach the subject from a self-centered viewpoint. Self-help books, even Christian ones, usually offer the same predictable steps to finding your life's purpose: Consider your dreams. Clarify your values. Set some goals. Figure out what you are good at. Aim high. Go for it! Be disciplined. Believe you can achieve your goals. Involve others. Never give up.

Of course, these recommendations often lead to great success. You can usually succeed in reaching a goal if you put your mind to it. But being successful and fulfilling your life's purpose are *not at all* the same issue! You could reach all your personal goals, becoming a raving success by the world's standard, and *still* miss the purposes for which God created you. You need more than self-help advice. The Bible says, "Self-help is no help at all. Self-sacrifice is the way, my way, to finding yourself, your true self."[3]

This is not a self-help book. It is not about finding the right career, achieving your dreams, or planning your life. It is not about how to cram more activities into an overloaded schedule. Actually, it will teach you how to do *less* in life—by focusing on what matters most. It is about becoming what *God* created you to be.

How, then, do you discover the purpose you were created for? You have only two options. Your first option is *speculation*. This is what most people choose. They conjecture, they guess, they theorize. When people say, "I've always thought life is...," they mean, "This is the best guess I can come up with."

> *You were made by God and for God—and until you understand that, life will never make sense.*

For thousands of years, brilliant philosophers have discussed and speculated about the meaning of life. Philosophy is an important subject and has its uses, but when it comes to determining the purpose of life, even the wisest philosophers are just guessing.

Dr. Hugh Moorhead, a philosophy professor at Northeastern Illinois University, once wrote to 250 of the best-known philosophers, scientists, writers, and intellectuals in the world, asking them, "What is the meaning of life?" He then published their responses in a book. Some offered their best guesses, some admitted that they just made up a purpose for life, and others were honest enough to say they were clueless. In fact, a number of famous intellectuals asked Professor Moorhead to write back and tell them if he discovered the purpose of life![4]

Fortunately, there is an alternative to speculation about the meaning and purpose of life. It's *revelation*. We can turn to what God has revealed about life in his Word. The easiest way to discover the purpose of an invention is to ask the creator of it. The same is true for discovering your life's purpose: Ask God.

God has not left us in the dark to wonder and guess. He has clearly revealed his five purposes for our lives through the Bible. It is our Owner's Manual, explaining why we are alive, how life works, what to avoid, and what to expect in the future. It explains what no self-help or philosophy book could know. The Bible says, "God's wisdom... goes deep into the interior of his purposes...It's not the latest message, but more like the oldest—what God determined as the way to bring out his best in us."[5]

God is not just the starting point of your life; he is the source of it. To discover your purpose in life you must turn to God's Word, not the world's wisdom. You must build your life on eternal truths, not pop psychology, success-motivation, or inspirational stories. The Bible says, "It's in Christ that we find out who we are and what we are living for. Long before we first heard of Christ and got our hopes up, he had his eye on us, had designs on us for glorious living, part of the overall purpose he is working out in everything and everyone."[6] This verse gives us three insights into your purpose.

1. You discover your identity and purpose through a relationship with Jesus Christ. If you don't have such a relationship, I will later explain how to begin one.

2. God was thinking of you long before you ever thought about him. His purpose for your life predates your conception. He planned it before you existed, *without your input!* You may choose your career, your spouse, your hobbies, and many other parts of your life, but you don't get to choose your purpose.

3. The purpose of your life fits into a much larger, cosmic purpose that God has designed for eternity. That's what this book is about.

Andrei Bitov, a Russian novelist, grew up under an atheistic Communist regime. But God got his attention one dreary day. He recalls, "In my twenty-seventh year, while riding the metro in Leningrad (now St. Petersburg) I was overcome with a despair so great that life seemed to stop at once, preempting the future entirely, let alone any meaning. Suddenly, all by itself, a phrase appeared: *Without God life makes no sense.* Repeating it in astonishment, I rode the phrase up like a moving staircase, got out of the metro and walked into God's light."[7]

You may have felt in the dark about *your* purpose in life. Congratulations, you're about to walk into the light.

```
─────────── Day One ───────────
        Thinking about My Purpose

            Point to Ponder:
            It's not about me.

          Verse to Remember:
"Everything got started in him and finds its purpose in him."
              Colossians 1:16b (Msg)

          Question to Consider:
In spite of all the advertising around me, how can I remind
myself that life is really about living for God, not myself?
```

1. Job 12:10 (TEV).
2. Romans 8:6 (Msg).
3. Matthew 16:25 (Msg).
4. Hugh S. Moorhead, comp., *The Meaning of Life According to Our Century's Greatest Writers and Thinkers* (Chicago: Chicago Review Press, 1988).
5. 1 Corinthians 2:7 (Msg).
6. Ephesians 1:11 (Msg).
7. David Friend, ed., *The Meaning of Life* (Boston: Little, Brown, 1991), 194.

YOU ARE NOT AN ACCIDENT

Rick Warren

I am your Creator. You were in my care even before you were born.
ISAIAH 44:2A (CEV)

God doesn't play dice.
ALBERT EINSTEIN

You are not an accident.

Your birth was no mistake or mishap, and your life is no fluke of nature. Your parents may not have planned you, but God did. He was not at all surprised by your birth. In fact, he expected it.

Long before you were conceived by your parents, you were conceived in the mind of God. He thought of you first. It is not fate, nor chance, nor luck, nor coincidence that you are breathing at this very moment. You are alive because God wanted to create you! The Bible says, "The Lord will fulfill his purpose for me."[1]

God prescribed every single detail of your body. He deliberately chose your race, the color of your skin, your hair, and every other feature. He custom-made your body just the way he wanted it. He also determined the natural talents you would possess and the uniqueness of your personality. The Bible says, "You know me inside and out, you know every bone in my body; You know exactly how I was made, bit by bit, how I was sculpted from nothing into something."[2]

Because God made you for a reason, he also decided *when* you would be born and *how long* you would live. He planned the days of your life in advance, choosing the exact time of your birth and death. The Bible says, "You saw me before I was born and scheduled each day of my life before I began to breathe. Every day was recorded in your Book!"[3]

God also planned *where* you'd be born and where you'd live for his purpose. Your race and nationality are no accident. God left no detail to chance. He planned it all for *his* purpose. The Bible says,

"From one man he made every nation,...and he determined the times set for them and the exact places where they should live."[4] Nothing in your life is arbitrary. It's all for a purpose.

> Long before you were conceived by your parents, you were conceived in the mind of God.

Most amazing, God decided *how* you would be born. Regardless of the circumstances of your birth or who your parents are, God had a plan in creating you. It doesn't matter whether your parents were good, bad, or indifferent. God knew that those two individuals possessed *exactly* the right genetic makeup to create the custom "you" he had in mind. They had the DNA God wanted to make you.

While there are illegitimate parents, there are no illegitimate children. Many children are unplanned by their parents, but they are not unplanned by God. God's purpose took into account human error, and even sin.

God never does anything accidentally, and he never makes mistakes. He has a reason for everything he creates. Every plant and every animal was planned by God, and every person was designed with a purpose in mind. God's motive for creating you was his love. The Bible says, "Long before he laid down earth's foundations, he had us in mind, had settled on us as the focus of his love."[5]

God was thinking of you even *before* he made the world. In fact, that's why he created it! God designed this planet's environment just so we could live in it. We are the focus of his love and the most valuable of all his creation. The Bible says, "God decided to give us life through the word of truth so we might be the most important of all the things he made."[6] This is how much God loves and values you!

God is not haphazard; he planned it all with great precision. The more physicists, biologists, and other scientists learn about the universe, the better we understand how it is uniquely suited for our existence, custom-made with the *exact* specifications that make human life possible.

Dr. Michael Denton, senior research fellow in human molecular genetics at the University of Otago in New Zealand, has concluded, "All the evidence available in the biological sciences supports the core proposition...that the cosmos is a specially designed whole with life and mankind as its fundamental goal and purpose, a whole in which all facets of reality have their meaning and explanation in this central fact."[7] The Bible said the same thing thousands of years earlier: "God formed the earth...He did not create it to be empty but formed it to be inhabited."[8]

Why did God do all this? Why did he bother to go to all the trouble of creating a universe for us? Because he is a God of love. This kind of love is difficult to fathom, but it's fundamentally reliable. You were created as a special object of God's love! God made you so he could love you. This is a truth to build your life on.

The Bible tells us, "God is love."[9] It doesn't say God *has* love. He *is* love! Love is the essence of God's character. There is perfect love in the fellowship of the Trinity, so God didn't *need* to create you. He wasn't lonely. But he wanted to make you in order to express his love. God says, "I have carried you since you were born; I have taken care of you from your birth. Even when you are old, I will be the same. Even when your hair has turned gray, I will take care of you. I made you and will take care of you."[10]

If there was no God, we would all be "accidents," the result of astronomical random chance in the universe. You could stop reading this book, because life would have no purpose or meaning or significance. There would be no right or wrong, and no hope beyond your brief years here on earth.

But there *is* a God who made you for a reason, and your life has profound meaning! We discover that meaning and purpose *only* when we make God the reference point of our lives. The Message paraphrase of Romans 12:3 says, "The only accurate way to understand ourselves is by what God is and by what he does for us."

This poem by Russell Kelfer sums it up:

> You are who you are for a reason.
> You're part of an intricate plan.
> You're a precious and perfect unique design,
> Called God's special woman or man.
> You look like you look for a reason.
> Our God made no mistake.

He knit you together within the womb,
You're just what he wanted to make.
The parents you had were the ones he chose,
And no matter how you may feel,
They were custom-designed with God's plan in mind,
And they bear the Master's seal.
No, that trauma you faced was not easy.
And God wept that it hurt you so;
But it was allowed to shape your heart
So that into his likeness you'd grow.
You are who you are for a reason,
You've been formed by the Master's rod.
You are who you are, beloved,
Because there is a God![11]

Day Two
Thinking about My Purpose

Point to Ponder:
I am not an accident.

Verse to Remember:
*"I am your Creator. You were in my care
even before you were born."* Isaiah 44:2 (CEV)

Question to Consider:
*Knowing that God uniquely created me,
what areas of my personality, background, and physical
appearance am I struggling to accept?*

---

1. Psalm 138:8a (NIV).
2. Psalm 139:15 (Msg).
3. Psalm 139:16 (lb).
4. Acts 17:26 (NIV).
5. Ephesians 1:4a (Msg).
6. James 1:18 (NCV).
7. Michael Denton, *Nature's Destiny: How the Laws of Biology Reveal Purpose in the Universe* (New York: Free Press, 1998), 389.
8. Isaiah 45:18 (GWT).
9. 1 John 4:8
10. Isaiah 46:3–4 (NCV)
11. Russell Kelfer. Used by permission.

WHAT DRIVES YOUR LIFE?

Rick Warren

I observed that the basic motive for success is the
driving force of envy and jealousy!
ECCLESIASTES 4:4 (LB)

The man without a purpose is like a ship without a rudder—
a waif, a nothing, a no man.
THOMAS CARLYLE

Everyone's life is driven by something.

Most dictionaries define the verb *drive* as "to guide, to control, or to direct." Whether you are driving a car, a nail, or a golf ball, you are guiding, controlling, and directing it at that moment. What is the driving force in your life?

Right now you may be driven by a problem, a pressure, or a deadline. You may be driven by a painful memory, a haunting fear, or an unconscious belief. There are hundreds of circumstances, values, and emotions that can drive your life. Here are five of the most common ones:

Many people are driven by guilt. They spend their entire lives running from regrets and hiding their shame. Guilt-driven people are manipulated by memories. They allow their past to control their future. They often unconsciously punish themselves by sabotaging their own success. When Cain sinned, his guilt disconnected him from God's presence, and God said, "You will be a restless wanderer on the earth."[1] That describes most people today—wandering through life without a purpose.

We are products of our past, but we don't have to be prisoners of it. God's purpose is not limited by your past. He turned a murderer named Moses into a leader and a coward named Gideon into a courageous hero, and he can do amazing things with the rest of your life, too.

God specializes in giving people a fresh start. The Bible says, "What happiness for those whose guilt has been forgiven!...What relief for those who have confessed their sins and God has cleared their record."[2]

Many people are driven by resentment and anger. They hold on to hurts and never get over them. Instead of releasing their pain through forgiveness, they rehearse it over and over in their minds. Some resentment-driven people *"clam up"* and internalize their anger, while others *"blow up"* and explode it onto others. Both responses are unhealthy and unhelpful.

Resentment always hurts you more than it does the person you resent. While your offender has probably forgotten the offense and gone on with life, you continue to stew in your pain, perpetuating the past.

Listen: Those who have hurt you in the past cannot continue to hurt you now unless you hold on to the pain through resentment. Your past is past! Nothing will change it. You are only hurting yourself with your bitterness. For your own sake, learn from it, and then let it go. The Bible says, "To worry yourself to death with resentment would be a foolish, senseless thing to do."[3]

Many people are driven by fear. Their fears may be a result of a traumatic experience, unrealistic expectations, growing up in a high-control home, or even genetic predisposition. Regardless of the cause, fear-driven people often miss great opportunities because they're afraid to venture out. Instead they play it safe, avoiding risks and trying to maintain the status quo.

Fear is a self-imposed prison that will keep you from becoming what God intends for you to be. You must move against it with the weapons of faith and love. The Bible says, "Well-formed love banishes fear. Since fear is crippling, a fearful life—fear of death, fear of judgment—is one not yet fully formed in love."[4]

Many people are driven by materialism. Their desire to acquire becomes the whole goal of their lives. This drive to always want more is based on the misconceptions that having more will make me more happy, more important, and more secure, but all three ideas are untrue. Possessions only provide *temporary* happiness. Because things do not change, we eventually become bored with them and then want newer, bigger, better versions.

It's also a myth that if I get more, I will be more important. Self-worth and net worth are not the same. Your value is not determined by your valuables, and God says the most valuable *things* in life are not things!

The most common myth about money is that having more will make me more secure. It won't. Wealth can be lost instantly through a variety of uncontrollable factors. Real security can only be found in that which can never be taken from you—your relationship with God.

Many people are driven by the need for approval. They allow the expectations of parents or spouses or children or teachers or friends to control their lives. Many adults are still trying to earn the approval of unpleasable parents. Others are driven by peer pressure, always worried by what others might think. Unfortunately, those who follow the crowd usually get lost in it.

I don't know all the keys to success, but one key to failure is to try to please everyone. Being controlled by the opinions of others is a guaranteed way to miss God's purposes for your life. Jesus said, "No one can serve two masters."[5]

> *Nothing matters more than knowing God's purposes for your life, and nothing can compensate for not knowing them.*

There are other forces that can drive your life but all lead to the same dead end: unused potential, unnecessary stress, and an unfulfilled life.

This forty-day journey will show you how to live a *purpose-driven* life—a life guided, controlled, and directed by God's purposes. Nothing matters more than knowing God's purposes for your life, and nothing can compensate for not knowing them—not success, wealth, fame, or pleasure. Without a purpose, life is motion without meaning, activity without direction, and events without reason. Without a purpose, life is trivial, petty, and pointless.

The Benefits of Purpose-Driven Living

There are five great benefits of living a purpose-driven life:

Knowing your purpose gives meaning to your life. We were made to have meaning. This is why people try dubious methods, like astrology or psychics, to discover it. When life has meaning, you can bear almost anything; without it, nothing is bearable.

A young man in his twenties wrote, "I feel like a failure because I'm struggling to become something, and I don't even know what it is. All I know how to do is to get by. Someday, if I discover my purpose, I'll feel I'm beginning to live."

Without God, life has no purpose, and without purpose, life has no meaning. Without meaning, life has no significance or hope. In the Bible, many different people expressed this hopelessness. Isaiah complained, "I have labored to no purpose; I have spent my strength in vain and for nothing."[6] Job said, "My life drags by—day after hopeless day"[7] and "I give up; I am tired of living. Leave me alone. My life makes no sense."[8] The greatest tragedy is not death, but life without purpose.

Hope is as essential to your life as air and water. You need hope to cope. Dr. Bernie Siegel found he could predict which of his cancer patients would go into remission by asking, "Do you want to live to be one hundred?" Those with a deep sense of life purpose answered yes and were the ones most likely to survive. Hope comes from having a purpose.

If you have felt hopeless, hold on! Wonderful changes are going to happen in your life as you begin to live it on purpose. God says, "I know what I am planning for you...'I have good plans for you, not plans to hurt you. I will give you hope and a good future.'"[9] You may feel you are facing an impossible situation, but the Bible says, "God ...is able to do far more than we would ever dare to ask or even dream of—infinitely beyond our highest prayers, desires, thoughts, or hopes."[10]

Knowing your purpose simplifies your life. It defines what you do and what you don't do. Your purpose becomes the standard you use to evaluate which activities are essential and which aren't. You simply ask, "Does this activity help me fulfill one of God's purposes for my life?"

Without a clear purpose you have no foundation on which you base decisions, allocate your time, and use your resources. You will tend to make choices based on circumstances, pressures, and your mood at that moment. People who don't know their purpose try to do too much—and *that* causes stress, fatigue, and conflict.

It is impossible to do everything people want you to do. You have just enough time to do God's will. If you can't get it all done, it means you're trying to do more than God intended for you to do (or, possibly, that you're watching too much television). Purpose-driven living leads to a simpler lifestyle and a saner schedule. The Bible says, "A pretentious, showy life is an empty life; a plain and simple life is a full life."[11] It also leads to peace of mind: "You, Lord, give perfect peace to those who keep their purpose firm and put their trust in you."[12]

Knowing your purpose focuses your life. It concentrates your effort and energy on what's important. You become effective by being selective.

It's human nature to get distracted by minor issues. We play *Trivial Pursuit* with our lives. Henry David Thoreau observed that people live lives of *"quiet desperation,"* but today a better description is *aimless distraction.* Many people are like gyroscopes, spinning around at a frantic pace but never going anywhere.

Without a clear purpose, you will keep changing directions, jobs, relationships, churches, or other externals—hoping each change will settle the confusion or fill the emptiness in your heart. You think, *Maybe this time it will be different,* but it doesn't solve your real problem —a lack of focus and purpose.

The Bible says, "Don't live carelessly, unthinkingly. Make sure you understand what the Master wants."[13]

The power of focusing can be seen in light. Diffused light has little power or impact, but you can concentrate its energy by focusing it. With a magnifying glass, the rays of the sun can be focused to set grass or paper on fire. When light is focused even more as a laser beam, it can cut through steel.

There is nothing quite as potent as a focused life, one lived on purpose. The men and women who have made the greatest difference in history were the most focused. For instance, the apostle

> *If you want your life to have impact, focus it!*
> 🦋

Paul almost single-handedly spread Christianity throughout the Roman Empire. His secret was a focused life. He said, "I am focusing all my energies on this one thing: Forgetting the past and looking forward to what lies ahead."[14]

If you want your life to have impact, focus it! Stop dabbling. Stop trying to do it all. Do less. Prune away even good activities and do only that which matters most. Never confuse activity with productivity. You can be busy without a purpose, but what's the point? Paul said, "Let's keep focused on that goal, those of us who want everything God has for us."[15]

Knowing your purpose motivates your life. Purpose always produces passion. Nothing energizes like a clear purpose. On the other hand, passion dissipates when you lack a purpose. Just getting out of bed becomes a major chore. It is usually meaningless work, not overwork, that wears us down, saps our strength, and robs our joy.

George Bernard Shaw wrote, "This is the true joy of life: the being used up for a purpose recognized by yourself as a mighty one; being a force of nature instead of a feverish, selfish little clot of ailments and grievances, complaining that the world will not devote itself to making you happy."

> *You weren't put on earth to be remembered. You were put here to prepare for eternity.*

Knowing your purpose prepares you for eternity. Many people spend their lives trying to create a lasting legacy on earth. They want to be remembered when they're gone. Yet, what ultimately matters most will not be what others say about your life but what *God* says. What people fail to realize is that all achievements are eventually surpassed, records are broken, reputations fade, and tributes are forgotten. In college, James Dobson's goal was to become the school's tennis champion. He felt proud when his trophy was prominently placed in the school's trophy cabinet. Years later, someone mailed him that trophy. They had found it in a trashcan when the school was remodeled. Jim said, *"Given enough time, all your trophies will be trashed by someone else!"*

Living to create an earthly legacy is a short-sighted goal. A wiser use of time is to build an *eternal* legacy. You weren't put on earth to be remembered. You were put here to prepare for eternity.

One day you will stand before God, and he will do an audit of your life, a final exam, before you enter eternity. The Bible says, "Remember, each of us will stand personally before the judgment seat of God...Yes, each of us will have to give a personal account to God."[16] Fortunately, God wants us to pass this test, so he has given us the questions in advance. From the Bible we can surmise that God will ask us two crucial questions:

First, *"What did you do with my Son, Jesus Christ?"* God won't ask about your religious background or doctrinal views. The only thing that will matter is, did you accept what Jesus did for you and did you learn to love and trust him? Jesus said, "I am the way and the truth and the life. No one comes to the Father except through me."[17]

Second, *"What did you do with what I gave you?"* What did you do with your life—all the gifts, talents, opportunities, energy, relationships, and resources God gave you? Did you spend them on yourself, or did you use them for the purposes God made you for?"

Preparing you for these two questions is the goal of this book. The first question will determine where you spend eternity. The second question will determine what you do in eternity. By the end of this book you will be ready to answer both questions.

Day Three
Thinking about My Purpose

Point to Ponder:
Living on purpose is the path to peace.

Verse to Remember:
"You, Lord, give perfect peace to those
who keep their purpose firm and put their trust in you."
Isaiah 26:3 (TEV)

Questions to Consider:
What would my family and friends say is the
driving force of my life? What do I want it to be?

---

1. Genesis 4:12 (NIV).
2. Psalm 32:1 (lb).
3. Job 5:2 (TEV).
4. 1 John 4:18 (Msg).
5. Matthew 6:24 (NLT).
6. Isaiah 49:4 (NIV).
7. Job 7:6 (lb).
8. Job 7:16 (TEV).
9. Jeremiah 29:11 (NCV).
10. Ephesians 3:20 (lb).
11. Proverbs 13:7 (Msg).
12. Isaiah 26:3 (TEV).
13. Ephesians 5:17 (Msg).
14. Philippians 3:13 (NLT).
15. Philippians 3:15 (Msg).
16. Romans 14:10b, 12 (NLT).
17. John 14:6 (NIV).

WE SHALL MORPH INDEED

The Hope of Transformation

John Ortberg

Now, with God's help, I shall become myself.
SØREN KIERKEGAARD

I could not quiet that pearly ache in my heart
that I diagnosed as the cry of home.
PAT CONROY

I am disappointed with myself. I am disappointed not so much with particular things I have done as with aspects of who I have become. I have a nagging sense that all is not as it should be.

Some of this disappointment is trivial. I wouldn't have minded getting a more muscular physique. I can't do basic home repairs. So far I haven't shown much financial wizardry.

Some of this disappointment is neurotic. Sometimes I am too concerned about what others think of me, even people I don't know.

Some of this disappointment, I know, is worse than trivial; it is simply the sour fruit of self-absorption. I attend a high school reunion and can't choke back the desire to stand out by looking more attractive or having achieved more impressive accomplishments than my classmates. I speak to someone with whom I want to be charming, and my words come out awkward and pedestrian. I am disappointed in my ordinariness. I want to be, in the words of

> *I am disappointed with myself...I have a nagging sense that all is not as it should be.*

Garrison Keillor, named "Sun-God, King of America, Idol of Millions, Bringer of Fire, The Great Haji, Thun-Dar the Boy Giant."

But some of this disappointment in myself runs deeper. When I look in on my children as they sleep at night, I think of the kind of father I want to be. I want to create moments of magic, I want them to remember laughing until the tears flow, I want to read to them and make the books come alive so they love to read, I want to have slow, sweet talks with them as they're getting ready to close their eyes, I want to sing them awake in the morning. I want to chase fireflies with them, teach them to play tennis, have food fights, and hold them and pray for them in a way that makes them feel cherished.

I look in on them as they sleep at night, and I remember how the day really went: I remember how they were trapped in a fight over checkers and I walked out of the room because I didn't want to spend the energy needed to teach them how to resolve conflict. I remember how my daughter spilled cherry punch at dinner and I yelled at her about being careful as if she'd revealed some deep character flaw; I yelled at her even though I spill things all the time and no one yells at me; I yelled at her—to tell the truth—simply because I'm big and she's little and I can get away with it. And then I saw that look of hurt and confusion in her eyes, and I knew there was a tiny wound on her heart that I had put there, and I wished I could have taken those sixty seconds back. I remember how at night I didn't have slow, sweet talks, but merely rushed the children to bed so I could have more time to myself. I'm disappointed.

And it's not just my life as a father. I am disappointed also for my life as a husband, friend, neighbor, and human being in general. I think of the day I was born, when I carried the gift of promise, the gift given to all babies. I think of that little baby and what might have been: the ways I might have developed mind and body and spirit, the thoughts I might have had, the joy I might have created.

I am disappointed that I still love God so little and sin so much. I always had the idea as a child that adults were pretty much the people they wanted to be. Yet the truth is, I am embarrassingly sinful. I am capable of dismaying amounts of jealousy if someone succeeds more visibly than I do. I am disappointed at my capacity to be small and petty. I cannot pray for very long without my mind drifting into a fantasy of angry revenge over some past slight I thought I had long since forgiven or some grandiose fantasy of achievement. I can convince people I'm busy and productive and yet waste large amounts of time watching television.

These are just some of the disappointments. I have other ones, darker ones, that I'm not ready to commit to paper. The truth is, even to write these words is a little misleading, because it makes me sound more sensitive to my fallenness than I really am. Sometimes, although I am aware of how far I fall short, it doesn't even bother me very much. And I am disappointed at my lack of disappointment.

Where does this disappointment come from? A common answer in our day is that it is a lack of self-esteem, a failure to accept oneself. That may be part of the answer, but it is not the whole of it, not by a long shot. The older and wiser answer is that the feeling of disappointment is not the problem, but a reflection of a deeper problem—my failure to be the person God had in mind when he created me. It is the "pearly ache" in my heart to be at home with the Father.

Universal Disappointment

One of the most profound statements I have heard about the human condition was one I first encountered when I was only five years old. It was spoken by my hero, Popeye the Sailor Man. When he was frustrated or wasn't sure what to do or felt inadequate, Popeye would simply say, "I yam what I yam."

Popeye was not a sophisticated guy. He had never been in therapy and was woefully out of touch with his shadow self and his inner child. He did not have much education as far as we know. He knew who he was: a simple, sea-faring, pipe-smoking, Olive Oyl-loving sailor man, and he wouldn't pretend to be anything else. He "owned his story," as Lewis Smedes puts it. "I yam what I yam."

But I always thought there was a note of sadness in Popeye's expression. It was generally offered as an explanation of his shortcomings. It does not anticipate much growth or change. It doesn't leave him much of a shot at getting to be what he yam not. "Don't get your hopes up," he seemed to say. "Don't expect too much. I yam what I yam—and [he would add in his bleakest moments] that's all that I yam."

That is the sad cry of the human race. You have said those words, in your own way, and so have I. This is the struggle between disappointment and hope.

Dis-appointing God

The word itself is apt: I am in a state of dis-appointment. I am missing the life that I was appointed by God to live—missing my

> *I am in a state of dis-appointment. I am missing the life that I was appointed by God to live.*

calling. And I have dis-appointed God. I have removed him from the central role he longs to play in my life; I have refused to "let God be God" and have appointed myself in his place. I yam what I yam.

But that's not all that I am. I am called to become the person God had in mind when he originally designed me. This is what is behind Kierkegaard's wonderful prayer, "And now Lord, with your help I shall become myself." This book is about spiritual growth. It is about that holy and mysterious process described by the apostle Paul when he said he was "in the pain of childbirth until Christ is formed in you." The goal of such growth is to live as if Jesus held unhindered sway over our bodies. Of course, it is still *we* doing the living. We are called by God to live as our uniquely created selves—our temperament, our gene pool, our history. But to grow spiritually means to live increasingly as Jesus would in our unique place—to perceive what Jesus would perceive if he looked through our eyes, to think what he would think, to feel what he would feel, and therefore to do what he would do.

The goal of this book is to help us to grow spiritually. But it is hard to write about spiritual formation in a way that captures the urgency of the subject. Too often people think about their "spiritual lives" as just one more aspect of their existence, alongside and largely separate from their "financial lives" or their "vocational lives." Periodically they may try to "get their spiritual lives together" by praying more regularly or trying to master another spiritual discipline. It is the religious equivalent of going on a diet or trying to stick to a budget.

The truth is that the term *spiritual life* is simply a way of referring to one's life—every moment and facet of it—from God's perspective. Another way of saying it is this: God is not interested in your "spiritual life." God is just interested in your life. He intends to redeem it.

From The Life You've Always Wanted *by John Ortberg*

God's Work of Art

One of the great works of art in the Western world is Michelangelo's *Pietà*, a marble statue of an anguished Mary holding the crucified Christ. Some years ago a fanatic nationalist rushed upon the masterpiece and began smashing it with a sledgehammer. Although the damage was significant, Vatican artists were able to restore the statue to near-perfect condition.

You were created to be a masterpiece of God. Paul writes, "For we are God's *poiemma*"—a word that can mean God's "workmanship," or even God's "work of art." God made you to know oneness with him and with other human beings. God made you to be co-regent with him—to "fill the earth and subdue it," to "have dominion" over creation under his reign and with his help. It is the goodness of God's work in creating us that makes our fallenness so tragic. This is why my disappointment in myself runs so deep.

But God is determined to overcome the defacing of his image in us. His plan is not simply to repair *most* of our brokenness. He wants to make us new creatures. So the story of the human race is not just one of universal disappointment, but one of inextinguishable hope.

Inextinguishable Hope and the Gospel

Frederick Buechner once wrote that every age has produced fairy tales. Something inside us believes, or wants to believe, that the world as we know it is not the whole story. We long for the reenchantment of reality. We hope that death is not the end, that the universe is something more than an enclosed terrarium. So we keep spinning and repeating stories that hold the promise of another world.

But these stories don't simply demand that another world exists. A common feature of fairy tales is that the enchanted world is not far away. You step into a wardrobe and you're in Narnia. You walk through a forest and stumble on a cottage with seven dwarfs. This other world turns out to be far closer than you thought.

In fact, the stories that endure are the ones that most deeply touch this longing inside us. Buechner quotes J. R. R. Tolkien:

> It is the mark of the good fairy-story, of the higher
> or more complete kind, that however wild its events,
> however fantastic or terrible the adventures, it can give
> to the child or man that hears it, when the "turn" comes,
> a catch of the breath, a beat and lifting of the heart,
> near to (or indeed accompanied by) tears, as keen as
> that given by any form of literary art.

Furthermore, fairy tales are not just stories about the transformation of the world around us. They are usually about the transformation of the central characters: frogs becoming princes, ugly ducklings becoming swans, wooden marionettes becoming real boys. George MacDonald gives to his hero, Curdie, the magical gift of being able to tell by the touch of someone's hand what he or she is turning into.

These are all features, Buechner says, that the gospel has in common with fairy tales, with this one great difference: The gospel is true.

Jesus' announcement of the gospel is simply the announcement of the existence and availability of another dimension of existence, another world. "The kingdom of God has come near," he said. "Repent, and believe in the good news." The Good News—the word we translate "gospel"—is that this fallen world as we know it is not the whole story. There is another realm. It is as real as the chair I sit in and the book you read.

> *The story of the human race is not just one of universal disappointment, but one of inextinguishable hope.*

These words of Jesus announce the great "turn" in the history of the world. The lid is off the terrarium. Anytime someone heard Jesus say them—really heard them—these words would bring a catch of the breath, a beating and uplifting of the heart, and sometimes tears. They still do.

The good news is especially that this world—the kingdom of God —is closer than you think. It is available to ordinary men and women. It is available to people who have never thought of themselves as religious or spiritual. It is available to you. You can live in it—now.

This means in part that your story is the story of transformation. You will not always be as you are now; the day is coming when you will be something incomparably better—or worse.

C. S. Lewis expressed that hope this way:

> It is a serious thing to live in a society of possible gods
> and goddesses, to remember that the dullest and most
> uninteresting person you can talk to may one day be
> a creature which, if you saw it now, you would be
> strongly tempted to worship, or else a horror and a
> corruption such as you now meet, if at all, only in
> a nightmare. All day long we are, in some degree,
> helping each other to one or other of these destinations.
> ...There are no ordinary people. You have never talked
> to a mere mortal. Nations, cultures, arts, civilizations—
> these are mortal, and their life is to ours as the life of
> a gnat. But it is immortals whom we joke with, work
> with, marry, snub, and exploit—immortal horrors or
> everlasting splendors.

This is why Jesus came. This is what spiritual life is about. This is your calling—to become what Lewis calls an "everlasting splendor."

The Need to "Turn Aside"

God holds out the possibility of transformation. One day when the human race had not heard a word of hope for a long time, a man named Moses walked past a shrub. He had seen it before, perhaps a hundred times. Only this time it was different. This time the "turn" comes; this time the wardrobe opens into Narnia; this time the bush is on fire with the presence of God.

And Moses said, "I must turn aside and look at this great sight, and see why the bush is not burned up." Everything turned on Moses' being willing to "turn aside"—to interrupt his daily routine to pay attention to the presence of God. He didn't have to. He could have looked the other way, as many of us would. He would have just missed the Exodus, the people of Israel, his calling, the reason for his existence. He would have missed knowing God.

But he didn't miss it. He stopped. He "turned aside."

God said he wanted to begin a new community of human existence, and he wanted Moses to lead it. He wanted

> *Moses had seen the shrub before, perhaps a hundred times. Only this time it was different.*

Moses to go to Pharaoh, the commander-in-chief of a superpower, and tell him that his vast Israelite labor force is no longer available.

But God's sense of timing seemed strange to Moses. Forty years ago maybe—forty years ago he was young and strong and the product of the greatest education the advanced civilization of Egypt could produce. Forty years ago he had powerful connections and high hopes. But now he was a nobody, an anonymous shepherd in a forgotten desert, rejected by his own people and a fugitive from the Egyptians.

"Who am I that I should go to Pharaoh?" Moses asked. "Nobody knows me. I am slow of speech and slow of tongue. I am disappointed in myself. I yam what I yam."

God said to Moses what he has said to you and me and millions of other Moseses: "I know all about that. It doesn't really matter much. For *I* will be with you. Your guilt and your inadequacies are no longer the ultimate truth about you. *You are what you are—but that's not all that you are. You are what you are, but you are not yet what you will be.* I will be with you."

To which Moses responded, logically enough: "Who are you? What if I go to the people and tell them the God of our fathers has sent me, and they ask me his name—what should I tell them?"

And God answered: "I am what I am." God wanted to be known intimately, by name. This same God had already been active in human history, ready to transform anyone then or now who is willing to turn aside before a burning bush: "I am the God of Abraham and Sarah, of Isaac and Rebekah; I am the God who cares for my people. I have seen the misery of my children when they thought I was not looking. I have heard their groans when they thought I was not listening. I am the God who saw you in the reeds when you were hidden, in the desert when you fled as a fugitive." For this is the God who hides in burning bushes and speaks in a still small voice.

"Get your hopes up!" God says. "You know me. I yam what I yam."

Transformation the Goal

A few years ago, the dominant interest of six-year-olds in the United States was a group of teenage superheroes called the Mighty

Morphin Power Rangers. The shows were an unlikely hit—originally produced on a very low budget in Japan, then badly dubbed into English.

The key to the show's appeal was the characters' ability to "morph." Ordinarily they were normal adolescents, but as needed they could access a power beyond themselves to become martial arts heroes for justice. Their rallying cry in moments of crisis was "It's morphing time!" and they would be transformed with the ability to do extraordinary things.

The show became such a huge hit that the term *morph* has begun creeping into magazine articles and everyday conversations and may become part of our permanent vocabulary. It became a standard phrase around our house if someone was in need of serious attitude adjustment: "It's morphing time."

Of course, it is not just six-year-olds who want to morph. The desire for transformation lies deep in every human heart. This is why people enter therapy, join health clubs, get into recovery groups, read self-help books, attend motivational seminars, and make New Year's resolutions.

> *The possibility of transformation is the essence of hope.*

The possibility of transformation is the essence of hope. Psychologist Aaron Beck says that the single belief most toxic to a relationship is the belief that the other person cannot change.

This little word *morph* has a long history. It actually comes from one of the richest Greek words in the New Testament, and in a sense this little word is the foundation of this whole book. *Morphoo* means "the inward and real formation of the essential nature of a person." It was the term used to describe the formation and growth of an embryo in a mother's body.

Paul used this word in his letter to the Galatians: "...until Christ is *formed* in you." He agonized until Christ should be born in those people, until they should express his character and goodness in their whole being. Paul said they—like us—are in a kind of spiritual gestation process. We are pregnant with possibilities of spiritual growth and moral beauty so great that they cannot be adequately described as anything less than the formation of Christ in our very lives.

Paul used another form of this word when he told the Christians in Rome that God had predestined them to be "conformed to the image of his Son." This word, *summorphizo*, means to have the same form as another, to shape a thing into a durable likeness. Spiritual growth is a molding process: We are to be to Christ as an image is to the original.

Still another form of the word appears in Romans when Paul says we are not to be conformed to the world around us but *"transformed* by the renewing of your minds." This word is *metamorphoo*, from which comes the English word *metamorphosis*. A creeping caterpillar is transformed into a soaring butterfly—yet as the children of God we are to undergo a change that makes that one barely noticeable.

When morphing happens, I don't just do the things Jesus would have done; I find myself *wanting* to do them. They appeal to me. They make sense. I don't just go around trying to do right things; I *become* the right sort of person.

These are audacious statements. Ordinary people can receive power for extraordinary change. It's morphing time, Paul says.

To help people remember this, I developed a little liturgy at a church I served. I would say to the congregation, "It's morphing time." They would reply, "We shall morph indeed."

The primary goal of spiritual life is human transformation. It is not making sure people know where they're going after they die, or helping them have a richer interior life, or seeing that they have lots of information about the Bible, although these can be good things. Let's put first things first. The first goal of spiritual life is the reclamation of the human race. It's morphing time.

Not only that, but this goal can be pursued full-time. For a long time in my own life a very bad thing happened: I had reduced my "tools for spiritual growth" to a few activities such as prayer and Bible study or a few periods of the day called a quiet time. I took an embarrassingly long time to learn that every moment of my life is an opportunity to learn from God how to live like Jesus, how to live in the kingdom of God. I had to discover that there are practical, concrete ways to help me "turn aside." Elizabeth Barrett Browning wrote:

Earth's crammed with Heaven,
And every common bush afire with God,
But only he who sees takes off his shoes—
The rest sit round it and pluck blackberries.

The purpose of this book is to help you learn how to use every moment, every activity of life, for morphing purposes.

A Case Study: The Morphing of Mabel

It can be helpful to see how God brings about transformation in the lives of ordinary people, so I would like to introduce you to a friend of a friend of mine. Her name is Mabel. This is what my friend, Tom Schmidt, wrote:

"The state-run convalescent hospital is not a pleasant place. It is large, understaffed, and overfilled with senile and helpless and lonely people who are waiting to die. On the brightest of days it seems dark inside, and it smells of sickness and stale urine. I went there once or twice a week for four years, but I never wanted to go there, and I always left with a sense of relief. It is not the kind of place one gets used to.

"On this particular day I was walking in a hallway that I had not visited before, looking in vain for a few who were alive enough to receive a flower and a few words of encouragement. This hallway seemed to contain some of the worst cases, strapped onto carts or into wheelchairs and looking completely helpless.

"As I neared the end of this hallway, I saw an old woman strapped up in a wheelchair. Her face was an absolute horror. The empty stare and white pupils of her eyes told me that she was blind. The large hearing aid over one ear told me that she was almost deaf. One side of her face was being eaten by cancer. There was a discolored and running sore covering part of one cheek, and it had pushed her nose to one side, dropped one eye, and distorted her jaw so that what should have been the corner of her mouth was the bottom of her mouth. As a consequence, she drooled constantly. I was told later that when new nurses arrived, the supervisors would send them to feed this woman, thinking that if they could stand this sight they could stand anything in the building. I also learned later that this woman was eighty-nine years old and *that she had been here, bedridden, blind, nearly deaf, and alone, for twenty-five years.* This was Mabel.

"I don't know why I spoke to her—she looked less likely to respond than most of the people I saw in that hallway. But I put a flower in her hand and said, 'Here is a flower for you. Happy Mother's Day.' She held the flower up to her face and tried to smell it, and then she spoke. And much to my surprise, her words, although somewhat garbled because of her deformity, were obviously produced by a clear mind. She said, 'Thank you. It's lovely. But can I give it to someone else? I can't see it, you know, I'm blind.'

"I said, 'Of course,' and I pushed her in her chair back down the hallway to a place where I thought I could find some alert patients. I found one, and I stopped the chair. Mabel held out the flower and said, 'Here, this is from Jesus.'

"That was when it began to dawn on me that this was not an ordinary human being. Later I wheeled her back to her room and learned more about her history. She had grown up on a small farm that she managed with only her mother until her mother died. Then she ran the farm alone until 1950 when her blindness and sickness sent her to the convalescent hospital. For twenty-five years she got weaker and sicker, with constant headaches, backaches, and stomachaches, and then the cancer came too. Her three roommates were all human vegetables who screamed occasionally but never talked. They often soiled their bedclothes, and because the hospital was understaffed, especially on Sundays when I usually visited, the stench was often overpowering.

"Mabel and I became friends over the next few weeks, and I went to see her once or twice a week for the next three years. Her first words to me were usually an offer of hard candy from a tissue box near her bed. Some days I would read to her from the Bible, and often when I would pause she would continue reciting the passage from memory, word-for-word. On other days I would take a book of hymns and sing with her, and she would know all the words of the old songs. For Mabel, these were not merely exercises in memory. She would often stop in mid-hymn and make a brief comment about lyrics she considered particularly relevant to her own situation. I never heard her speak of loneliness or pain except in the stress she placed on certain lines in certain hymns.

"It was not many weeks before I turned from a sense that I was being helpful to a sense of wonder, and I would go to her with a pen and paper to write down the things she would say...

"During one hectic week of final exams I was frustrated because my mind seemed to be pulled in ten directions at once with all of the things that I had to think about. The question occurred to me, 'What does Mabel have to think about—hour after hour, day after day, week after week, not even able to know if it's day or night?' So I went to her and asked, 'Mabel, what do you think about when you lie here?'

"And she said, 'I think about my Jesus.'

"I sat there, and thought for a moment about the difficulty, for me, of thinking about Jesus for even five minutes, and I asked, 'What do you think about Jesus?' She replied slowly and deliberately as I wrote..:

> I think about how good he's been to me. He's been awfully good to me in my life, you know...I'm one of those kind who's mostly satisfied...Lots of folks wouldn't care much for what I think. Lots of folks would think I'm kind of old-fashioned. But I don't care. I'd rather have Jesus. He's all the world to me.

"And then Mabel began to sing an old hymn:

> Jesus is all the world to me,
> My life, my joy, my all.
> He is my strength from day to day,
> Without him I would fall.
> When I am sad, to him I go,
> No other one can cheer me so.
> When I am sad He makes me glad.
> He's my friend.

"*This is not fiction.* Incredible as it may seem, a human being really lived like this. I know. I knew her. *How could she do it?* Seconds ticked and minutes crawled, and so did days and weeks and months and years of pain without human company and without an explanation of why it was all happening—and she lay there and sang hymns. *How could she do it?*

"The answer, I think, is that Mabel had something that you and I don't have much of. She had power. Lying there in that bed, unable to move, unable to see, unable to hear, unable to talk to anyone, she had incredible power."

Here was an ordinary human being who received supernatural power to do extraordinary things. Her entire life consisted of following Jesus as best she could in her situation: patient endurance of suffering, solitude, prayer, meditation on Scripture, worship, fellowship when it was possible, giving when she had a flower or a piece of candy to offer.

Imagine being in her condition and saying, "I think about how good he's been to me. He's been awfully good to me in my life, you know...I'm one of those kind who's mostly satisfied." This is the Twenty-third Psalm come to life: "The Lord is my shepherd, I shall not want."

For anyone who really saw Mabel—who was willing to "turn aside"—a hospital bed became a burning bush; a place where this ordinary and pain-filled world was visited by the presence of God. When others saw the life in that hospital bed, they wanted to take off their shoes. The lid was off the terrarium. Then the turn came, with a catch of the breath, and a beating of the heart, and tears. They were standing on holy ground.

> Here was an ordinary human being who received supernatural power to do extraordinary things.

Do you believe such a life is possible for an ordinary human being? Do you believe it is possible for you? This is promised in the gospel— the Good News proclaimed by Jesus: "The kingdom of God has come near; repent, and believe in the good news." The good news as Jesus preached it is that now it is possible for ordinary men and women to live in the presence and under the power of God. The good news as Jesus preached it is not about the minimal entrance requirements for getting into heaven when you die. It is about the glorious redemption of human life—your life.

It's morphing time.

Sources

Kierkegaard: Søren Kierkegaard, *The Prayers of Kierkegaard*, ed. Perry LeFevre. Chicago: University of Chicago Press, Chicago, 1956, 147. (page 21)

Conroy: Pat Conroy, *Beach Music*. New York: Doubleday, 1995. (page 21)

Keillor: Garrison Keillor, *Lake Wobegon Days*. New York: Penguin Books, 1986, 323. (page 21)

Smedes: Lewis B. Smedes, *Shame and Grace*. San Francisco: Harper Collins, 1993, 145. (page 23)

Kierkegaard: Kierkegaard, *The Prayers of Kierkegaard*, 147. (page 24)

"The pain of childbirth": Galatians 4:19. (page 24)

"God's workmanship": Ephesians 2:10 niv. (page 25)

"Fill the earth": Genesis 1:28. (page 25)

Buechner: Frederick Buechner, *Telling the Truth: The Gospel as Tragedy, Comedy, and Fairy Tale*. San Francisco: Harper & Row, 1977. (page 25)

Tolkien: J. R. R. Tolkien, quoted in Buechner, *Telling the Truth*, 82. (page 26)

MacDonald: George MacDonald, *The Princess and Curdie*. Baltimore: Puffin Books, 1976. (page 26)

Buechner: Buechner, *Telling the Truth*. (page 26)

"The kingdom of God": Mark 1:15. (page 26)

Lewis: C. S. Lewis, *The Weight of Glory*. New York: Macmillan, 1980, 11. (page 27)

"I must turn aside": Exodus 3 passim. (page 27)

"I am slow of speech": See Exodus 4:10. (page 28)

Beck: Aaron Beck, *Love Is Not Enough*. New York: Harper & Row, 1988. See discussion on 155ff. (page 29)

"Until Christ is formed": Galatians 4:19. (page 29)

"Conformed to the image": Romans 8:29. (page 30)

"Transformed by the renewing": Romans 12:2. (page 30)

Browning: Elizabeth Barrett Browning, *Aurora Leigh*, Book vii, Line 820. (page 31)

Schmidt: Tom Schmidt, *Trying to be Good*. Grand Rapids: Zondervan, 1990, 180–83. Used by permission. (page 31)

"Jesus is all the world": Words and music by Will Lamartine Thompson (1847–1909). (page 33)

"The Lord is my shepherd": Psalm 23:1. (page 34)

SURPRISED BY CHANGE

The Goal of Spiritual Life

John Ortberg

If you are weary of some sleepy form of devotion,
probably God is as weary of it as you are.
FRANK LAUBACH

"Spirituality" wrongly understood or pursued is a major
source of human misery and rebellion against God.
DALLAS WILLARD

The Man Who Never Changed

Hank, as we'll call him, was a cranky guy. He did not smile easily, and when he did, the smile often had a cruel edge to it, coming at someone's expense. He had a knack for discovering islands of bad news in oceans of happiness. He would always find a cloud where others saw a silver lining.

Hank rarely affirmed anyone. He operated on the assumption that if you compliment someone, it might lead to a swelled head, so he worked to make sure everyone stayed humble. His was a ministry of cranial downsizing.

His native tongue was complaint. He carried judgment and disapproval the way a prisoner carries a ball and chain. Although he went to church his whole life, he was never unshackled.

A deacon in the church asked him one day, "Hank, are you happy?"

Hank paused to reflect, then replied without smiling, "Yeah."

"Well, tell your face," the deacon said. But so far as anybody knows, Hank's face never did find out about it.

Occasionally, Hank's joylessness produced unintended joy for others.

There was a period of time when his primary complaints centered around the music in the church. "It's too loud!" Hank protested—to the staff, the deacons, the ushers, and eventually the innocent visitors to the church.

We finally had to take Hank aside and explain that complaining to complete strangers was not appropriate and he would have to restrict his laments to a circle of intimate friends. And that was the end of it. So we thought.

A few weeks later, a secretary buzzed me on the intercom to say that an agent from OSHA—the Occupational Safety and Health Administration—was here to see me. "I'm here to check out a complaint," he said. As I tried to figure out who on the staff would have called OSHA over a church problem, he began to talk about decibel levels at airports and rock concerts.

"Excuse me," I said, "are you sure this was someone on the church staff that called?"

"No," he explained. "If anyone calls—whether or not they work here—we're obligated to investigate."

Suddenly the light dawned: Hank had called OSHA and said, "The music at my church is too loud." And they sent a federal agent to check it out.

By this time the rest of the staff had gathered in my office to see the man from OSHA.

"We don't mean to make light of this," I told him, "but nothing like this has ever happened around here before."

"Don't apologize," he said. "Do you have any idea how much ridicule I've faced around my office since everyone discovered I was going out to bust a church?"

Sometimes Hank's joylessness ended in comedy, but more often it produced sadness. His children did not know him. His son had a wonderful story about how he met his wife at a dance, but he never told his father because Hank did not approve of dancing.

Hank could not effectively love his wife or his children or people outside his family. He was easily irritated. He had little use for the poor, and a casual contempt for those whose accents or skin pigment differed from his own. Whatever capacity he once might have had for joy or wonder or gratitude atrophied. He critiqued and judged and complained, and his soul got a little smaller each year.

Do We Expect Transformation?

Hank was not changing. He was once a cranky young guy, and he grew up to be a cranky old man. But even more troubling than his lack of change was the fact that *nobody was surprised by it*. It was as if everyone simply expected that his soul would remain withered and sour year after year, decade after decade. No one seemed bothered by the condition. It was not an anomaly that caused head-scratching bewilderment. No church consultants were called in. No emergency meetings were held to probe the strange case of this person who followed the church's general guidelines for spiritual life and yet was nontransformed.

The church staff did have some expectations. We expected that Hank would affirm certain religious beliefs. We expected that he would attend services, read the Bible, support the church financially, pray regularly, and avoid certain sins. But here's what we didn't expect: *We didn't expect that he would progressively become the way Jesus would be if he were in Hank's place*. We didn't assume that each year would find him a more compassionate, joyful, gracious, winsome personality. We didn't anticipate that he was on the way to becoming a source of delight and courtesy who overflowed with "rivers of living water." So we were not shocked when it didn't happen. We would have been surprised if it did!

Most of us want to be changed, to become more like Christ. But is it happening? According to a Gallup poll, nine of ten Americans say they pray daily, and 84 million Americans—almost a third of the population—say they have made a personal commitment to Christ as Savior. But as William Iverson writes, "A pound of meat would surely be affected by a quarter pound of salt. If this is real Christianity, the 'salt of the earth,' where is the effect of which Jesus spoke?"

Because by and large we do not expect people to experience ongoing transformation, we are not led to question whether perhaps the standard prescriptions for spiritual growth being given in the church are truly adequate to lead people into a transformed way of life.

> *We were not shocked when change didn't happen. We would have been surprised if it did!*

I believe we need to say that this state of affairs is simply not acceptable. It is not God's plan for his community. As C. S. Lewis said in another context, we are "like an ignorant child who wants to go on making mud pies in a slum because he cannot imagine what is meant by the offer of a holiday at the sea. We are far too easily pleased."

In fact, Hank's problem is not just that he is failing to change. His problem—and the problem of all of us who become "far too easily pleased"—is that we may end up changing in ways that leave us worse off than before.

The Danger of "Pseudo-Transformation"

The great danger that arises when we don't experience authentic transformation is that we will settle for what might be called *pseudo-transformation*. We know that as Christians we are called to "come out and be separate," that our faith and spiritual commitment should make us different somehow. But if we are not marked by greater and greater amounts of love and joy, we will inevitably look for substitute ways of distinguishing ourselves from those who are not Christians. This deep pattern is almost inescapable for religious people: If we do not become changed from the inside-out—if we don't morph—we will be tempted to find external methods to satisfy our need to feel that we're different from those outside the faith. If we cannot be transformed, we will settle for being informed or conformed.

Boundary-Marker Spirituality

James Dunn notes that in the first century a.d. a vast amount of rabbinic writing focused on circumcision, dietary laws, and Sabbath keeping. This seems odd, because no devout rabbi would have said these matters were at the heart of the Law.
They knew its core: "Hear, O Israel: The Lord is our God, the Lord alone. You shall love the Lord your God with all your heart, and with all your soul, and with all your might." So why the focus on these three practices?

The answer involves what might be called "identity" or "boundary markers." Groups have a tendency to be exclusive. Insiders want to separate themselves from outsiders. So they adopt boundary markers. These are highly visible, relatively superficial practices—matters of vocabulary or dress or style—whose purpose is to *distinguish* between those inside a group and those who are outside.

For example, imagine that you were driving through the Haight-Asbury district of San Francisco in the 1960s. If you came to a stoplight and a Volkswagen van pulled up next to you, plastered with peace signs and "Make Love Not War" bumper stickers and driven by a long-haired, tie-dyed, granny-glasses wearer, you would have known you were driving next to a hippie. If it were the 1980s and you were to see a BMW with a driver wearing Gucci shoes, a Rolex watch, and moussed hair and nibbling on brie, you would know you were driving next to a yuppie. Bikers, too, are recognizable by their preference in fashion color (black), fabric (leather), skin ornamentation (tattoo), and beverage of choice ("great taste, less filling"). Farmers and doctors and politicians and rock stars all have their own ways of distinguishing who is in their fraternity or sorority.

With this in mind, the importance of circumcision, dietary laws, and Sabbath keeping in the first century becomes clear. These were the boundary markers; the highly visible, relatively superficial practices that allowed people to distinguish who was inside and who was outside the family of God. What is worse, the insiders become proud and judgmental toward outsiders. They practiced what might be called a "boundary-oriented approach" to spiritual life: Just look at people and you will know who are the sheep and who are the goats. This is pseudo-transformation.

Spiritual Life Defined by Its Center

With Jesus it was not so. Jesus brought a message that spoke to the deepest longings of the human heart to become not simply conformed to a religious subculture but transformed into "new creatures." Instead of focusing on the boundaries, Jesus focused on the center, the heart of spiritual life. When asked to identify what the law is about, Jesus' response was simply "Love God, love people." He named a fundamentally different way of identifying who are the children of God: "Do they love God, and do they love the people who mean so much to him?"

Jesus' early followers understood this clearly. The apostle Paul wrote to the church at Corinth about the significance of having many spiritual "markers" but lacking the center: "If I speak in the tongues of mortals and of angels, but do not have love, I am a noisy gong or a clanging cymbal. And if I have prophetic powers, and understand all mysteries and all knowledge, and if I have all faith, so as to remove mountains, but do not have love, I am nothing." John put it even more bluntly: "Everyone who loves is born of God and knows God. Whoever does not love *does not know God*, for God is love."

This is why the religious leaders of Jesus' day so often fought with him about circumcision, dietary laws, and the Sabbath. Jesus was not just disagreeing with them on how to interpret the Law. He was *threatening their very understanding of themselves as the people of God.*

Boundary Markers in Our Day

The search for identity markers did not die out in the first century. The church I grew up in was a fine church, and I am deeply in its debt, but we also had our own set of markers there. The senior pastor could have been consumed with pride or resentment, but as long as his preaching was orthodox and the church was growing, his job would probably not be in jeopardy. But if some Sunday morning he had been smoking a cigarette while greeting people after the service,

> *Instead of focusing on the boundaries, Jesus focused on the center, the heart of spiritual life.*

he would not have been around for the evening service. Why? No one at the church would have said that smoking a single Camel was a worse sin than a life consumed with pride and resentment. But for us, cigarette-smoking became an identity marker. It was one of the ways we were able to tell the sheep from the goats.

That is why the marker held an emotional charge far beyond its theological significance. For the pastor to smoke a cigarette would have caused a scandal, not because we were so naive that we thought it an evil thing to do, but because it would have violated an unspoken boundary marker. It would have threatened our sense of identity.

Of course, many beliefs and values will inevitably divide those who choose to follow Christ from those who don't. Jesus himself said he came not "to bring peace, but a sword." But what makes something a boundary marker is its being seized upon by the group as an opportunity to reinforce a false sense of superiority, fed by the intent to exclude others.

Religious boundary markers change from generation to generation. The Christian college I attended in the late seventies still had in effect a rule against the performance of jazz music on campus, a regulation instituted in the early twentieth century. Fifty years later, no one was willing to rescind it for fear of appearing to compromise essential beliefs. The irony is that students were perfectly free to listen to punk rock or heavy metal—but Louis Armstrong was off- limits. On Sundays the tennis courts were locked up, but for some reason the volleyball court was left accessible. As a tennis player, I always maintained that volleyball was the more worldly of the two sports, as it was more closely associated with California and was often played on the beach.

If you give it much thought, whether your religious background is liberal or conservative, Protestant or Catholic, you can probably come up with your own set of identity markers.

A boundary-oriented approach to spirituality focuses on people's position: Are you inside or outside the group? A great deal of energy is spent clarifying what counts as a boundary marker.

But Jesus consistently focused on people's *center*: Are they oriented and moving *toward* the center of spiritual life (love of God and people), or are they moving *away from it*? This is why he shocked people by saying that many religious leaders—who observed all the recognized boundary markers—were in fact outside the kingdom of God. They were—like Hank—increasingly dead to love. And this is why Jesus could say that "the tax collectors and the prostitutes" who were a million miles away from the religious subculture, but who had turned, converted, and oriented themselves toward God and love, were already in the kingdom.

This was the great irony of his day: The "righteous" were more damaged by their righteousness than the sinners were by their sin.

The Distortion of Spirituality

The misunderstanding of true spirituality has caused immense damage to the human race. Tragically, it is possible to think we are becoming more spiritual when in fact we are only becoming more smug and judgmental. Pseudo-transformation means becoming what Mark Twain once called "a good man in the worst sense of the word."

> *The misunderstanding of true spirituality has caused immense damage to the human race.* ❧

Winston Churchill, told that a political opponent of his by the name of Cripps—who was widely disliked for his smug self-righteousness—had just stopped smoking cigars, commented, "Too bad. Those cigars were his last contact with humanity." (Another time, the story goes, Churchill saw Cripps passing by and remarked, "There, but for the grace of God, goes God.")

Getting clear on what spiritual life looks like is no casual affair. This is life or death to the soul. Sheldon Van Auken wrote that the strongest argument for Christianity is Christians, when they are drawing life from God. The strongest argument against Christianity? Also Christians, when they become exclusive, self-righteous, and complacent.

Dallas Willard writes,

> How many people are radically and permanently repelled from The Way by Christians who are unfeeling, stiff, unapproachable, boringly lifeless, obsessive, and dissatisfied? Yet such Christians are everywhere, and what they are missing is the wholesome liveliness springing from a balanced vitality with the freedom of God's loving rule. . . . Spirituality wrongly understood or pursued is a major source of human misery and rebellion against God.

So how do I know if I am settling for pseudo-transformation instead of the real thing? In the gospel according to Matthew, Jesus offers a list of warning signs in capital letters. Here are a few that I find helpful.

1. Am I spiritually "inauthentic"?
"Woe to you. . . . For you clean the outside of the cup and of the plate, but inside they are full of greed and self-indulgence."

Inauthenticity involves a preoccupation with *appearing* to be spiritual.
Someone once asked me whether I thought that the church where I worked might be worldly.

"What do you mean by 'worldly'?" I asked him.

"Well, you use drama, and people are used to that in the world. And you play contemporary music just like they're used to hearing. So how will they know you're any different? Everybody knows that as Christians we're supposed to be different from people in the world by being more loving and more gentle, and everybody knows that we're not. So don't we have to do something to show we're different?"

In other words, if we can't be *holy*, shouldn't we at least be *weird*?

I act like that. I recently reread a letter I had written to a friend many years ago. Most of the letter was a review of current activities, and it sounded casual and natural. Then I wrote a few lines at the end about God and my spiritual life. But they didn't feel natural. They felt calculated and artificial, as if I were saying things I thought a spiritual person is *supposed* to say.

I realized I have a hard time even *talking* about God without trying to convince people I'm "spiritual." I try to hide my sin. I work harder at making people think I'm a loving person than I do at actually loving them.

A little boy went to Sunday school, where he knew the sort of answers you're supposed to give to questions. The teacher asked, "What is brown, furry, has a long tail, and stores up nuts for winter?"

"Well," the boy muttered, "I guess the answer is Jesus, but it sure sounds like a squirrel to me."

I act like that. I try to say spiritual-sounding things, even when I don't know what I'm saying: "I guess the answer is Jesus..."

2. Am I becoming judgmental or exclusive or proud?
"They love to have the place of honor at banquets and the best seats in the synagogues."

Pride is a potential problem for anyone who takes spiritual growth seriously. As soon as we start to pursue virtue, we begin to wonder why others aren't as virtuous as we are. The great mystic St. John of the Cross wrote:

> When beginners become aware of their own fervor and diligence in their spiritual works and devotional exercises, this prosperity of theirs gives rise to secret pride...they conceive a certain satisfaction in the contemplation of their works and of themselves... They condemn others in their heart when they see that they are not devout in their way.

Lee Strobel, my colleague at Willow Creek Community Church, is fond of quoting the reply Homer Simpson's fundamentalist neighbors gave when Homer asked them where they'd been: "We went away to a Christian camp. We were learning how to be more judgmental."

Where is that camp, and why is it so well attended?

I was in a small group with people I had just met, and immediately I found a little voice inside me categorizing everyone: "This one is needy and dependent—stay away. That one is bright and has much to offer—try to connect." Why do I constantly find myself *rating* people as if they were Olympic contestants and someone appointed me judge? Why do I so often *compare* myself with them as if we were in some kind of competition?

This tendency is one reason why God sometimes graciously hides our own growth from our eyes. Jean Caussade said that while God is always at work in us, many times his work "is formed, grows, and is accomplished *secretly* in souls without their *knowledge*."

3. Am I becoming more approachable, or less?
"They love . . . to have people call them rabbi."

In Jesus' day, lepers and prostitutes and tax collectors were especially careful to steer clear of the rabbis, who were considered especially close to God. The rabbis' had the mistaken notion that their spirituality required them to distance themselves from people. The irony is that the only rabbi the outcasts could touch turned out to be God himself.

Jesus was the most approachable person they had ever seen. The religious leaders had a kind of differentness that pushed people away. Jesus had a kind of differentness that drew people to him. True spirituality is that way.

4. Am I growing weary of pursuing spiritual growth?

"They tie up heavy burdens, hard to bear, and lay them on the shoulders of others."

The pursuit of righteousness is always an exhausting pursuit when it seeks a distorted goal. Steven Mosley speaks of how we trivialize goodness, becoming

> a "peculiar people" set at odd angles to the world rather than being an attractive light illuminating it. As a result, our morality calls out rather feebly. It whines from the corner of a sanctuary; it awkwardly interrupts pleasures; it mumbles excuses at parties; it shuffles along out of step and slightly behind the times...It's often regarded by our secular contemporaries as a narrow, even trivial, pursuit.

He captures the dynamic of the boundary-marker quest: "Tragically, conventional religious goodness manages to be both *intimidating* and *unchallenging* at the same time."

> *The pursuit of righteousness is always an exhausting pursuit when it seeks a distorted goal.*

"Both intimidating and unchallenging at the same time." This is the hallmark of spiritual life defined in terms of boundary markers. Intimidating—because it may involve thirty-nine separate rules about Sabbath keeping alone. Unchallenging—because we may devote our lives to observing all the rules and yet never open the heart to love or joy.

This is why people inside the church so often get weary. Observing boundary markers, conforming to a religious subculture, is simply not a compelling enough vision to captivate the human spirit. It was not intended to be.

5. Am I measuring my spiritual life in superficial ways?

"You blind guides! You strain out a gnat but swallow a camel!"

Suppose someone were to ask you, "How is your spiritual life going these days?" Quick—what's the first thing that comes to your mind?

For many years I thought about this only in terms of a few special activities. If someone asked me how my spiritual life was going, my first thought would be how I was doing at having a quiet time— praying and reading the Bible each day. If I had prayed and read the Bible for several consecutive prior days, I was likely to say that my spiritual life was going well. If not, I was likely to feel guilty and downcast. So prayer and Bible study became the gauge of my spiritual condition. As long as I did those two things I could go through the day confident of God's approval.

I often use a journal in these quiet times. But I discovered that sometimes when I was in a hurry and didn't really want to take time to be with God, I would still get out my journal and scribble a few sentences simply so I had an entry in it for that day. (I'm not sure why I did this. Did I think I was going to have to hand it in?) I found myself measuring my spiritual life by the regularity of journal entries. I even devised a strategy in case there was an embarrassingly long gap between entry dates: I could keep two journals and merely write in one: "See other journal."

But God's primary assessment of our lives is not going to be measured by the number of journal entries. I recently received a book of which the stated goal was to enable the reader to get up to "340 or 350 quiet times a year"—as if that were the point.

I suspect that if someone had asked the apostle Paul or the apostle John about his spiritual life, his first question would have been, "Am I growing in love for God and people?" The real issue is what kind of people we are becoming. Practices such as reading Scripture and praying are important—not because they prove how spiritual we are—but because God can use them to lead us into life. We are called to do nothing less than to experience day by day what Paul wrote to the church at Ephesus: "But God, who is rich in mercy, out of the great love with which he loved us even when we were dead through our trespasses, made us alive together with Christ."

Many years ago I took one of my daughters to see her first movie: *Snow White and the Seven Dwarfs*. For an hour and a half we lived in another world. I had forgotten how dark movies can be for a two-year-old. My daughter cried at the wicked stepmother, at the bite of the apple, at the coming of the curse.

My tears came at another place. Snow White was cleaning out the cottage and singing, "Someday, my prince will come." Suddenly it was as if it were my little girl on the screen, and I was thinking about the day when her "prince"—whoever that was to be—would come and she would go away and they would be together.

In that moment I had new empathy for the dwarfs. In this story they give their home and risk their lives for this foolish girl who eats the forbidden fruit and falls asleep and breaks their heart. And then the prince comes and awakens her with a kiss, and she runs off with him without a regret. But of course that is how it must be. That is her destiny.

And that is ours, too.

Each of us has tasted the forbidden fruit. We have all eaten the apple. We have all fallen under the curse. We are all, on our own, in a kind of living death.

But still the Prince comes, to bring freedom from the curse, life from death. Still the Prince comes, to kiss his bride. And every once in a while, somebody, somewhere, wakes up. And when that happens—that's life.

> "Sleeper, awake!
> Rise from the dead,
> and Christ will shine on you."

Sources

1. Laubach: Frank Laubach, "Game with Minutes," in *Man of Prayer*. Syracuse: Laubach Literacy International, 1990, 205. (page 37)

2. Willard: Dallas Willard, *The Spirit of the Disciplines*. San Francisco: Harper & Row, 1988, 81. (page 37)

3. Gallup poll: George Gallup and Jim Castelli, *The People's Religion: American Faith in the 90's*. New York: Macmillan, 1989. (page 39)

4. Iverson: William Iverson, in *Christianity Today*, 6 June 1980, 33. (page 39)

5. Lewis: C.S. Lewis, *The Weight of Glory*. New York: Macmillan, 1980, 4. (page 39)

6. Dunn: James Dunn, Romans 1–8, *Word Biblical Commentary*, vol.38. Dallas: Word Books, 1988. See especially his discussion of Paul and Pharisaic Judaism on lxiv–lxxii of the introduction. (page 40)

7. "Hear, O Israel": Deuteronomy 6:4–5. (page 40)

8. "Love God, love people": See Matthew 22:37–39. (page 41)

9. "If I speak": 1 Corinthians 13:1–2. (page 42)

10. "Everyone who loves": 1 John 4:7–8. (page 42)

11. "Not to bring peace": Matthew 10:34. (page 43)

12. "Tax collectors": Matthew 21:31. (page 43)

13. Twain: Mark Twain. Source unknown. (page 44)

14. Churchill: William Manchester, *The Last Lion: Winston Spencer Churchill*. New York: Bantam Books, 1983, 34. (page 44)

15. Van Auken: Sheldon Van Auken, *A Severe Mercy*. San Francisco: Harper & Row, 1977, 85. (page 44)

16. Willard: Willard, *The Spirit of the Disciplines*, 80, 91. (page 44)

17. "Woe to you": Matthew 23:25. (page 45)

18. "They love to have": Matthew 23:6. (page 45)

19. St. John of the Cross: St. *John of the Cross, The Dark Night of the Soul*. London: Harper Collins, 1995, 11. (page 46)

20. Simpson: From the weekly television program *The Simpsons*. (page 46)

21. Caussade: Jean Caussade, *The Sacrament of the Present Moment*. San Francisco:Harper &Row, 1987, 42. (page 46)

22. "They love ... to have": Matthew 23:6–7. (page 46)

23. "They tie up": Matthew 23:4. (page 47)

24. Mosley: *Steven Mosley, A Tale of Three Virtues*. Sisters, Ore.: Questar, 1989, 17. (page 47)

25. Mosley: Ibid., 19. (page 47)

26. "You blind guides!": Matthew 23:24. (page 47)

27. "But God, who is rich": Ephesians 2:4. (page 48)

28. "Sleeper, awake!": Ephesians 5:14. (page 49)

AN UNHURRIED LIFE

The Practice of "Slowing"

John Ortberg

People nowadays take time far more seriously than eternity.
THOMAS KELLY

Not long after moving to Chicago, I called a wise friend to ask for some spiritual direction. I described the pace at which things tend to move in my current setting. I told him about the rhythms of our family life and about the present condition of my heart, as best I could discern it. What did I need to do, I asked him, to be spiritually healthy?

Long pause.

"You must ruthlessly eliminate hurry from your life," he said at last. Another long pause.

"Okay, I've written that one down," I told him, a little impatiently. "That's a good one. Now what else is there?" I had many things to do, and this was a long-distance conversation, so I was anxious to cram as many units of spiritual wisdom into the least amount of time possible.

Another long pause.

"There is nothing else," he said.

He is the wisest spiritual mentor I have known. And while he doesn't know every detail about every grain of sin in my life, he knows quite a bit. And from an immense quiver of spiritual sagacity, he drew only one arrow. "There is nothing else," he said. "You must ruthlessly eliminate hurry from your life."

Imagine for a moment that someone gave you this prescription, with the warning that your life depends on it. Consider the possibility that perhaps your life does depend on it. Hurry is the great enemy of spiritual life in our day. Hurry can destroy our souls. Hurry can keep us from living well. As Carl Jung wrote, "Hurry is not of the devil; hurry is the devil."

> *The great danger is not that we will renounce our faith, but settle for a mediocre version of it.*

Again and again, as we pursue spiritual life, we must do battle with hurry. For many of us the great danger is not that we will renounce our faith. It is that we will become so distracted and rushed and preoccupied that we will settle for a mediocre version of it. We will just skim our lives instead of actually living them.

The Disease: Hurry Sickness

We suffer from what has come to be known as "hurry sickness." One of the great illusions of our day is that hurrying will buy us more time. I pulled into a service station recently where the advertising slogan read, "We help you move faster." But what if my primary need is not moving faster?

Time magazine noted that back in the 1960s, expert testimony was given to a subcommittee of the Senate on time management. The essence of it was that because of advances in technology, within twenty years or so people would have to radically cut back on how many hours a week they worked, or how many weeks a year they worked, or else they would have to start retiring sooner. The great challenge, they said, was what people would do with all their free time. Yet thirty years later, not many of us would say that our primary challenge in regard to time is what to do with all the excess.

We will buy anything that promises to help us hurry. The best-selling shampoo in America rose to the top because it combines shampoo and conditioner in one step, eliminating the need for all the time-consuming rinsing people used to have to do. Domino's became the No. 1 name in pizza because the company promised to deliver in thirty minutes or less. ("We don't sell pizza," said their CEO, "We sell delivery.") *USA Today* reports, "Taking a cue from Domino's Pizza, a Detroit hospital guarantees that emergency-room patients will be seen within 20 minutes—or treatment is free." The paper notes that since the offer was made, business has been up 30 percent at the hospital.

We worship at the shrine of the Golden Arches, not because they sell "good food," or even "cheap food," but because it is "fast food." Even after fast food was introduced, people still had to park their cars, go inside, order, and take their food to a table, all of which took time.

So we invented the Drive-Thru Lane to enable families to eat in vans, as nature intended.

Our world has become the world of the Red Queen in Alice in Wonderland: "Now here, you see, it takes all the running you can do, to keep in the same place. If you want to get somewhere else, you must run at least twice as fast as that!"

Ironically, all our efforts have not produced what we're after: a sense of what we might call "timefulness," a sense of having enough time. We often experience the opposite. Robert Banks notes that while American society is rich in goods, it is extremely time-poor. Many societies in the two-thirds world, by contrast, are poor in material possessions, by our standards, but they are rich in time. They are not driven or hurried. They live with a sense that there is adequate time to do what needs to be done each day.

Meyer Friedman defines hurry sickness as "above all, a continuous struggle and unremitting attempt to accomplish or achieve more and more things or participate in more and more events in less and less time, frequently in the face of opposition, real or imagined, from other persons." Hurry will keep us consumed by "the cares and riches and pleasures of life," as Jesus put it, and prevent his way from taking root in our hearts.

Jesus was quite aware of this kind of problem in his day. As we will see, he repeatedly withdrew from crowds and activities. He taught his followers to do likewise. When the disciples returned, their adrenaline pumping, from a busy time of ministry, Jesus told them, "Come away to a deserted place all by yourselves and rest a while." Mark explains that "many were coming and going, and they had no leisure even to eat." That could be the motto for some people today. Some people imagine this to be a good thing that perhaps God will reward one day: "What a life you had! You were even too busy to eat. Well done!"

But Mark did not mean this statement as a commendation. Jesus urged his disciples to take time out. Following Jesus cannot be done at a sprint. If we want to follow someone, we can't go faster than the one who is leading.

We must ruthlessly eliminate hurry from our lives. This does not mean we will never be busy. Jesus often had much to do, but he never did it in a way that severed the life-giving connection between him and his Father. He never did it in a way that interfered with his ability to give love when love was called for. He observed a regular practice of withdrawing from activity for the sake of solitude and prayer. Jesus was often busy, but never hurried.

Hurry is not just a disordered schedule. Hurry is a disordered heart.

Let's do a brief diagnostic exercise. How do we know if we are suffering from this hurry sickness? Here are some symptoms.

Constantly Speeding Up Daily Activities

If we have hurry sickness, we are haunted by the fear that there are just not enough hours in the day to do what needs to be done. We will read faster, talk faster, and when listening, nod faster to encourage the talker to accelerate. We will find ourselves chafing whenever we have to wait. At a stoplight, if there are two lanes and each contains one car, we will find ourselves guessing—based on the year, make, and model of each car—which one will pull away the fastest.

At a grocery store, if we have a choice between two check-out lines, we find ourselves counting how many people are in each line, multiplying this number by the number of items per cart. If we have really bad case of hurry sickness, then even after we get in line we keep track of the person who would have been me in the other line. If we get through and the person who would have been me is still waiting, we are elated. We've won. But if the alter-me is walking out of the store and we're still in line, we feel depressed. We have hurry sickness.

"Multiple-Tasking"

Despite all this rushing around, the hurry-sick person is still not satisfied. So out of the desperate need to hurry, we find ourselves doing or thinking more than one thing at a time. Psychologists speak of this as polyphasic activity; the more hopeful euphemism is multiple-tasking. (It could be called "doing more than one thing at a time," but that takes too long to say.) The car is a favorite place for this. Hurry-sick people may drive, eat, drink coffee, monitor the radio, shave or apply make-up, talk on the car phone, and make gestures—all at the same time. Or they may try to watch television, read, eat dinner, and carry on a conversation simultaneously.

Clutter

The lives of the hurry-sick lack simplicity. These people often carry around a time organizer the size of Montana. They keep acquiring stacks of books and magazines and then feel guilty for not reading them. They buy time-saving gadgets and don't have the time or patience to read the instructions and figure out how to use them.

Paul Pearsall writes that many of these types cannot seem to get rid of their "stuff." He advises,

You may require a "closet exorcist" experienced in dealing with the demons of closet clutter. . . . A trusted friend can also prevent the "restuffing phenomenon." Restuffing happens when, in the process of cleaning out closets and drawers, we somehow are stimulated to acquire new stuff.

There are other, less material forms of clutter. Life is cluttered when we are weighed down by the burden of all the things we have failed to say no to. Then comes the clutter of forgetting important dates, of missing appointments, of not following through.

Superficiality

"Superficiality is the curse of our age," writes Richard Foster. If Superficiality is our curse, then Hurry pronounces the spell. Depth always comes slowly.

This is simply a truth about human formation. Perhaps one reason that Abraham Lincoln achieved the depth of thought he did is that he grew up with so little to read. David Donald notes in his biography that Lincoln grew up

> *We have largely traded wisdom for information, depth for breadth. We want to microwave maturity.*

with access to very few books: the Bible, *Aesop's Fables* (which he virtually memorized), and a few others. "He must understand everything—even to the smallest thing—minutely and exactly," his stepmother remembered. "He would then repeat it over to himself again and again...and when it was fixed in his mind to suit him he never lost that fact or the understanding of it."

Lincoln himself often spoke of how slowly his mind worked, how even as an adult he read laboriously and out loud. His law partner and biographer William Herndon claimed that "Lincoln read less and thought more than any man in his sphere in America."

But today we have largely traded wisdom for information. We have exchanged depth for breadth. We want to microwave maturity.

An Inability to Love

The most serious sign of hurry sickness is a diminished capacity to love. Love and hurry are fundamentally incompatible. Love always takes time, and time is one thing hurried people don't have.

A pilot once told me his favorite airline story. An elderly couple were flying first class, sitting behind a businessman who was enormously frustrated with them. They had been just ahead of him in line at the gate, and again boarding the plane, and they moved slowly, but he was in a hurry. When the meal was served, they delayed the businessman again by having to get some pills from the overhead storage, inadvertently dropping a battered duffel bag. "What's the matter with you people?" he exploded, loudly enough for the whole cabin to hear. "I'm amazed you ever get anywhere. Why can't you just stay home?"

To register his anger, the man sat down and reclined his seat back as hard as he could—so hard that the elderly husband's tray of food spilled all over him and his wife. The flight attendant apologized to the couple profusely: "Is there anything we can do?" she asked. The husband explained it was their fiftieth wedding anniversary and they were flying for the first time. "Let me at least bring you a bottle of wine," the flight attendant offered.

She did so. When it was uncorked, the old husband stood up, proposed a toast—and poured the bottle over the head of the impatient businessman sitting in front of them.

And, the pilot told me, everybody in the cabin cheered.

Sunset Fatigue

Hurried people cannot love. Lewis Grant suggests we are afflicted with what he calls "sunset fatigue." When we come home at the end of a day's work, those who need our love the most, those to whom we are most committed, end up getting the leftovers. Sunset fatigue is when we are just too tired, or too drained, or too preoccupied, to love the people to whom we have made the deepest promises. Sunset fatigue has set in, Grant says, when

—you find yourself rushing even when there's no reason to;
—there is an underlying tension that causes sharp
    words or sibling quarrels;
—you set up mock races ("OK, kids, let's see who can
    take a bath fastest") that are really about your own
    need to get through it;
—you sense a loss of gratitude and wonder;
—you indulge in self-destructive escapes from fatigue:
    abusing alcohol, watching too much TV, listening
    to country western music [okay, the last one is
    mine, not Grant's].

It is because it kills love that hurry is the great enemy of spiritual life. Hurry lies behind much of the anger and frustration of modern life. Hurry prevents us from receiving love from the Father or giving it to his children. That's why Jesus never hurried. If we are to follow Jesus, we must ruthlessly eliminate hurry from our lives—because, by definition, we can't move faster than the one we are following.

We can do this: We can become unhurried people. We can become patient people.

Curing the Hurry Sickness

But we will not become unhurried on our own. We cannot achieve this alone. We will have to enter a life of training. So let's look at practices for the hurry-sick.

"Slowing"

The first practice is one we might call "slowing." This involves cultivating patience by deliberately choosing to place ourselves in positions where we simply have to wait. (This practice has a definite "gamelike" quality, although we may not like it much, at least at first.)

Over the next month deliberately drive in the slow lane on the expressway. It may be that not swerving from lane to lane will cause you to arrive five minutes or so later than you usually would. But you will find that you don't get nearly so angry at other drivers. Instead of trying to pass them, say a little prayer as they go by, asking God to bless them.

Declare a fast from honking. Put your horn under a vow of silence.

For a week, eat your food slowly. Force yourself to chew at least fifteen times before each swallow.

For the next month, when you are at the grocery store, look carefully to see which check-out line is the longest. Get in it. Let one person go ahead of you.

Go through one day without wearing a watch.

The list could go on, but you get the idea. We must find ways to deliberately choose waiting, ways that make hurry impossible. As we practice them, we should tell God we are trusting him to enable us to accomplish all we need to get done.

Often people worry that if they don't rush, they will accomplish less. In fact, researchers have found that there is simply no correlation between hurry or Type-A behavior and productivity.

We will discover we can survive without hurry. If we practice these ways diligently enough, we will become unhurried people.

The Need for Solitude

A more traditional practice is solitude. Jesus engaged in it frequently. At the beginning of his ministry, Jesus went to the wilderness for an extended period of fasting and prayer. He also went into solitude when he heard of the death of John the Baptist, when he was going to choose his disciples, after he had been involved in healing a leper, and after his followers had engaged in ministry. This pattern continued into the final days of his life, when again he withdrew into the solitude of the garden of Gethsemane to pray. He ended his ministry, as he began it, with the practice of solitude.

Jesus taught his followers to do the same. And as he said to them, "Come away to a deserted place," he says to us still. Wise followers of Christ's way have always understood the necessity and benefit of solitude. It is, to quote an old phrase, the "furnace of transformation."

What makes solitude so important? Solitude is the one place where we can gain freedom from the forces of society that will otherwise relentlessly mold us.

According to a much-traveled analogy, if we put a frog in a pot of boiling water, it will immediately hop out. But put the frog in water that's at room temperature and heat it slowly, and the creature will stay there until it boils to death. Put him in a lethal environment suddenly, and he will escape. But introduce the danger gradually, and he will never notice.

The truth is that the dangers to which we are most vulnerable are generally not the sudden, dramatic, obvious ones. They are the ones that creep up on us, that are so much a part of our environment that we don't even notice them.

The deeper truth is that we live in a lethal environment. American society is filled with ideas and values and pressures and temptations about success and security and comfort and happiness that we will not even notice unless we withdraw on occasion. Thomas Merton wrote that the early church fathers placed such a premium on solitude because they considered society to be a shipwreck from which any sane person must swim for his life. These people believed that to let oneself drift along, passively accepting the tenets and values of what they knew as society, was purely and simply a disaster. The apostle Paul put it this way: "Don't let the world around squeeze you into its own mold."

One writer notes an experiment done with mice a few years ago. A researcher found that it takes a high dose of amphetamines to kill a mouse living in solitude. But a group of mice will start hopping around and hyping each other up so much that a dosage twenty times smaller will be lethal—so great is the effect of "the world" on mice. In fact, a mouse that had been given no amphetamines at all, placed in a group on the drug, will get so hopped up that in ten minutes or so it will be dead. "In groups they go off like popcorn or firecrackers," the writer observed.

We might guess that only a mouse would be so foolish as to hang out with a bunch of other mice that were so hopped up, going at such a frantic pace in such mindless activity for no discernible purpose, that they would put their own well-being and even lives at risk. It would be wrong to think so. The messages come at us in a continual stream:

"We'll help you move faster...Act now, don't delay!...You can buy it now if you'll just stretch—no money down, easy monthly payments. ...You can earn it if you run a little faster, stay a little longer, work a little harder...It's okay to get old as long as you don't get wrinkled or gray or liver spots or bald—as long as you don't look old...It's okay to be frantic and stressed and empty and exhausted—that's the way everybody is...We'll help you move faster."

"The press of busyness is like a charm," Kierkegaard wrote. "Its power swells...it reaches out seeking always to lay hold of ever-younger victims so that childhood or youth are scarcely allowed the quiet and the retirement in which the Eternal may unfold a divine growth." The truth is, as much as we complain about it, we are drawn to hurry. It makes us feel important. It keeps the adrenaline pumping. It means we don't have to look too closely at the heart or life. It keeps us from feeling our loneliness.

Solitude is the remedy for the busyness that charms. But what exactly is solitude? What do we do when we practice solitude? What should we bring along to that quiet place?

The primary answer, of course, is "nothing." A man recently told me about preparing for his first extended period of solitude. He took books, message tapes, CDs, and a VCR—some of the very things we would think of trying to get away from.

At its heart, solitude is primarily about not doing something. Just as fasting means to refrain from eating, so solitude means to refrain from society. When we go into solitude, we withdraw from conversation, from the presence of others, from noise, from the constant barrage of stimulation.

> *At its heart, solitude is primarily about not doing something.*

"In solitude," Henri Nouwen wrote, "I get rid of my scaffolding." Scaffolding is all the stuff we use to keep ourselves propped up, to convince ourselves that we are important or okay. In solitude we have no friends to talk with, no phone calls or meetings, no television sets, no music or books or newspapers to occupy and distract the mind. Each of us would be, in the words of the old hymn, "just as I am." Neither accomplishments nor résumés nor possessions nor networks would define me—just me and my sinfulness, my desire or lack of desire for God.

Practicing Solitude

Solitude requires relentless perseverance. I find that unless I pull my calendar out and write down well in advance the times when I am committed to times of solitude, it won't happen.

I find it helpful to think about solitude in two categories. We need brief periods of solitude on a regular basis—preferably each day, even at intervals during the day. But we also need, at great intervals, extended periods of solitude—half a day, a day, or a few days.

We may want to begin a particular day by praying over the day's schedule—meetings to attend, tasks to perform, people we will be with—and placing it in God's hands. Through the day we could take five-minute breaks if that is possible, close the door to the office, and remind ourselves that one day the office and the building will be gone—but we will still belong to God.

Reviewing the Day with God

1. Be still for a moment and quiet your mind.
2. Acknowledge that Jesus is present. Invite him to teach you.
3. Go back in your mind to when you first woke up. Watch that scene, as if on video. This may lead you to pray for patience, greater love, courage, forgiveness, or other virtues.
4. Continue through the day, going from scene to scene. As you reflect on them, some scenes may fill you with gratitude, others with regret. Speak directly to the Lord about this. You may also be led to pray for some of the people you were inter acting with during the day.
5. End with a prayer of thanksgiving for God's mercy and love. Ask him to refresh you as you sleep.

At the end of the day it can be helpful to review the day with God: to go over the events that took place, to see what he might want to say to us through them, and to hand any anxieties or regrets over to him. The next page has a format that I find helpful.

For most, the best time to review a day is at bedtime, but if you are a confirmed morning person, you may want to do it when you first get up the next morning. A great benefit of this exercise is that we begin to learn from our days. When I was in athletics in school we used to watch videotapes of our performance. Watching the tapes was sometimes painful, yet worth it to be spared our making the same mistakes over and over.

The same idea holds here. When I began to practice solitude with this exercise, I discovered I experienced much more anger than I would ever have thought. I began to be aware of the attitudes and responses that were guiding my life.

Extended Solitude

I also need extended times alone. I try to withdraw for a day once a month or so, and sometime during the year I try to have a retreat for a couple of days. Retreat centers designed for such experiences are becoming more and more common, although any place where you can be undisturbed suffices.

Francis de Sales used the image of a clock to express his need for extended solitude.

> There is no clock, no matter how good it may be, that doesn't need resetting and rewinding twice a day, once in the morning and once in the evening. In addition, at least once a year it must be taken apart to remove the dirt clogging it, straighten out bent parts, and repair those worn out. In like manner, every morning and evening a man who really takes care of his heart must rewind it for God's service...Moreover, he must often reflect on his condition in order to reform and improve it. Finally, at least once a year he must take it apart and examine every piece in detail, that is every affection and passion, in order to repair whatever defects there may be.

Extended Solitude

1. Find a place where you can be uninterrupted and alone, such as a park or a retreat center.

2. Spend a brief time the night before to get ready, to ask God to bless the day, and to tell him you want to devote the day to him. This day is your gift to God, but even more, it is a gift God wants to give you. What do you need from the Lord: a sense of healing and forgiveness? Conviction for an apathetic heart? Compassion? A renewed sense of mission? Ask him for this.

3. Arrange the day around listening to God. The following format is adapted from Glandion Carney's book *The Spiritual Formation Toolkit.*

8:00–9:00 Prepare your mind and heart, take a walk, or do whatever will help you set aside concerns over tasks and responsibilities. Try to arrange your morning so you can remain in silence from the time you awaken.

9:00–11:00 Read and meditate on Scripture, taking time to stop to reflect when God seems to be speaking to you through the text.

11:00–12:00 Write down responses to what you have read. Speak to God about them.

12:00–1:00 Eat lunch and take a walk, reflecting on the morning.

1:00–2:00 Take a nap.

2:00–3:00 Set goals that emerge from the day's reflection.

3:00–4:00 Write down these goals and other thoughts in a journal. You may want to do this in the form of a letter to God. Prepare to re-enter society.

One of the great obstacles to extended solitude is that frequently it may feel like a waste of time. This may happen partly because we are conditioned to feel that our existence is justified only when we are doing something. But I believe this feeling comes also because our minds tend to wander. I used to think that if I devoted a large block of time to praying, I should be able to engage in solid, uninterrupted, focused prayer. But I can't. The first time I tried extended solitude, my mind wandered like a tourist with a Eurail pass. I would start praying, and the next thing I knew, I was immersed in an anger fantasy. In this fantasy someone who had hurt me was being deeply wounded by the wrong they had done me as I was righteously vindicated. Another time, after beginning to pray, I found myself the object of a success fantasy so grandiose that it would make Narcissus blush with modesty.

What I have come to realize, over time, is that brief times of focused prayer interspersed with these wanderings is all my mind is capable of at this point. One day I hope to do better. But for now, I find consolation in the words of Brother Lawrence: "For many years I was bothered by the thought that I was a failure at prayer. Then one day I realized I would always be a failure at prayer; and I've gotten along much better ever since."

You may be ready to try spending an extended period of time alone with God—perhaps a day. The first attempt at extended solitude can feel intimidating so some structure such as that described on the previous page may help.

Defeating Hurry Sickness

Sometime ago a newspaper in Tacoma, Washington, carried the story of Tattoo the basset hound. Tattoo didn't intend to go for an evening run, but when his owner shut his leash in the car door and took off for a drive, Tattoo had no choice. A motorcycle officer named Terry Filbert noticed a passing vehicle with something that appeared to be dragging behind it. As he passed the vehicle, he saw Tattoo. Officer Filbert finally chased the car to a stop, and Tattoo was rescued —but not before the dog reached a speed of twenty to thirty miles per hour and rolled over several times. He has not asked to go out for an evening walk for a long time.

There is too much Tattoo behavior going on in American society. There are too many people who spend their days going from one task to another. It is time to enter training for another way to live.

We must ruthlessly eliminate hurry from our lives.

Sources

1. Kelly: Thomas Kelly, *A Testament of Devotion*. New York: Harper Bros., 1941, 54. (page 51)

2. Jung: Carl Jung, quoted in Richard Foster, *Celebration of Discipline*. San Francisco: Harper & Row, 1978, 13. (page 51)

3. *Time*: Date unknown. (page 52)

4. *USA Today*: Date unknown. (page 52)

5. Carroll: Lewis Carroll, *Alice in Wonderland*. Reprint, Philadelphia: John H. Winston, 1957. (page 53)

6. Banks: Robert Banks, *All the Business of Life*. Claremont, Calif.: Albatross Books, 1987, 9. (page 53)

7. Friedman: Meyer Friedman and Diane Ulmer, *Treating Type A Behavior— And Your Heart*. New York: Fawcett Crest, 1984, 33. (page 53)

8. "The cares and riches": Luke 8:14. (page 53)

9. "Come away" and "many were coming": Mark 6:31. (page 53)

10. Pearsall: Paul Pearsall, *Super Joy*. New York: Doubleday, 1988, 134. (page 55)

11. Foster: Richard Foster, *Celebration of Discipline*. San Francisco: Harper & Row, 1978, 1. (page 55)

12. Donald: David Donald, *Lincoln*. New York: Simon & Schuster, 1995, 29. (page 55)

13. Herndon: William H. Herndon and Jesse E. Weik, *Herndon's Lincoln*. Chicago: Belford-Clarke Co., 1890, 477. (page 56)

14. Grant: Lewis Grant, quoted in Dolores Curren, *Traits of a Healthy Family*. New York: Ballantine, 1983. (page 57)

15. Researchers: Friedman and Ulmer, *Treating Type A Behavior—And Your Heart*, 179ff. (page 58)

16. Jesus in solitude: See, for example, Matthew 4:1ff.; 14:13; 14:23; 26:36ff. (page 58)

17. *Frog in boiling water:* The troubling aspect of this analogy, of course, is to wonder whether anyone has even tried it. What kind of sick-minded frog-hater would devise two methods for boiling frogs? How many other animals did he try it with first? Actually, a friend once sent me an article that featured interviews with Harvard biologists and an experiment involving an MIT research associate; it turns out that under test conditions the frog really did jump out of the gradually heated pot. So there you are. (page 59)

18. Merton: Thomas Merton, *The Wisdom of the Desert*. New York: New Directions, 1960, 3. (page 59)

19. "Don't let the world": Romans 12:2 Philipps. (page 59)

20. Mice on amphetamines: Cited in Dallas Willard, *The Spirit of the Disciplines*. San Francisco: Harper & Row, 1988, 160. (page 59)

21. Kierkegaard: Søren Kierkegaard, *Purity of Heart Is to Will One Thing*. New York: Harper & Row, 1956, 107. (page 60)

22. Nouwen: Henri Nouwen, *The Way of the Heart*. New York: Ballantine, 1981, 15. (page 60)

23. Francis: Francis de Sales, *Introduction to a Devout and Holy Life*. New York: Doubleday, 1989, 271. (page 62)

24. Carney: Glandion Carney and Coleman Moore, *The Spiritual Formation Toolkit*. Grand Rapids: CentrePointe, n.d. (page 63)

25. Brother Lawrence: Brother Lawrence, *The Practice of the Presence of God*. Springdale, Pa.: Whitaker House, 1982. See the fifth letter. (page 64)

MESSY

The Workshop of the Spiritual Life

Mike Yaconelli

I stake the future on the few humble and hearty lovers who
seek God passionately in the marvelous, messy world of
redeemed and related realities that lie in front of our noses.
WILLIAM MCNAMARA

Dear God,
I'm doing the best I can.
Frank
CHILDREN'S LETTERS TO GOD

I go into churches and everyone seems to feel
so good about themselves. Everyone calls themselves a
Christian nowadays. How dare we call ourselves Christians?
It's only for Jesus to decide whether we are Christian or not.
I don't think He's made a decision in my case, and I'm
afraid that when He does I am going to be sent straight to
hell. I don't feel I can call myself a Christian. I can't be satisfied with myself. We all seem to be pretty contented with
ourselves in church and that makes me sick. I think all this
contentment makes Jesus nervous.
ROBERT COLES, WITTENBURG DOOR

My life is a mess.

After forty-five years of trying to follow Jesus, I keep losing him
in the crowded busyness of my life. I know Jesus is there, somewhere,
but it's difficult to make him out in the haze of everyday life.

For as long as I can remember, I have wanted to be a godly
person. Yet when I look at the yesterdays of my life, what I see,
mostly, is a broken, irregular path littered with mistakes and failure.
I have had temporary successes and isolated moments of closeness
to God, but I long for the continuing presence of Jesus. Most of the
moments of my life seem hopelessly tangled in a web of obligations
and distractions.

I want to be a good person. I don't want to fail. I want to learn
from my mistakes, rid myself of distractions, and run into the arms

of Jesus. Most of the time, however, I feel like I am running away from Jesus into the arms of my own clutteredness.

I want desperately to know God better. I want to be consistent. Right now the only consistency in my life is my inconsistency. Who I want to be and who I am are not very close together. I am not doing well at the living-a-consistent-life thing.

I don't want to be St. John of the Cross or Billy Graham. I just want to be remembered as a person who loved God, who served others more than he served himself, who was trying to grow in maturity and stability. I want to have more victories than defeats, yet here I am, almost sixty, and I fail on a regular basis.

If I were to die today, I would be nervous about what people would say at my funeral. I would be happy if they said things like "He was a nice guy" or "He was occasionally decent" or "Mike wasn't as bad as a lot of people." Unfortunately, eulogies are delivered by people who know the deceased. I know what the consensus would be. "Mike was a mess."

When I was younger, I believed my inconsistency was due to my youth. I believed that age would teach me all I needed to know and that when I was older I would have learned the lessons of life and discovered the secrets of true spirituality.

I am older, a lot older, and the secrets are still secret from me.

I often dream that I am tagging along behind Jesus, longing for him to choose me as one of his disciples. Without warning, he turns around, looks straight into my eyes, and says, "Follow me!" My heart races, and I begin to run toward him when he interrupts with, "Oh, not you; the guy behind you. Sorry."

I have been trying to follow Christ most of my life, and the best I can do is a stumbling, bumbling, clumsy kind of following. I wake up most days with the humiliating awareness that I have no clue where Jesus is. Even though I am a minister, even though I think about Jesus every day, my following is...uh...meandering.

So I've decided to write a book about the spiritual life.

I know what you're thinking. Based on what I've just said about my walk with God, having me write about spirituality is like having Bozo the Clown explain the meaning of the universe, like playing

Handel's *Messiah* on the kazoo. How can someone whose life is obviously *unspiritual* presume to talk about spirituality? How can someone unholy presume to talk about holiness? It makes no sense.

Unless. Un*less!* Unless spirituality, as most of us understand it, is not spirituality at all.

Sadly, *spiritual* is most commonly used by Christians to describe people who pray all day long, read their Bibles constantly, never get angry or rattled, possess special powers, and have the inside track to God. *Spirituality*, for most, has an *other*worldly ring to it, calling to mind eccentric "saints" who have forsaken the world, taken vows of poverty, and isolated themselves in cloisters.

Nothing wrong with the spirituality of monks. Monks certainly experience a *kind* of spirituality, a way of seeking and knowing God, *but what about the rest of us?* What about those of us who live in the city, have a wife or husband, three children, two cats, and a washing machine that has stopped working? What about those of us who are single, work sixty to seventy hours a week, have parents who wonder why we're not married, and have friends who make much more money than we do? What about those of us who are divorced, still trying to heal from the scars of rejection, trying to cope with the single-parenting of children who don't understand why this has happened to them?

Is there a spirituality for the rest of us who are not secluded in a monastery, who don't have it all together and probably never will?

Spirituality for the Rest of Us

The answer is yes!

What landed Jesus on the cross was the preposterous idea that common, ordinary, broken, screwed-up people *could be godly!* What drove Jesus' enemies crazy were his criticisms of the "perfect" religious people and his acceptance of the imperfect nonreligious people. The shocking implication of Jesus' ministry is that *anyone* can be spiritual.

Scandalous? Maybe.

Maybe truth *is* scandalous. Maybe the scandal is that all of us are in some condition of not-togetherness, even those of us who are trying to be godly. Maybe we're all a mess, not only sinful messy but inconsistent messy, up-and-down messy, in-and-out messy, now-I-believe-now-I-don't messy, I-get-it-now-I-don't-get-it messy, I-understand-uh-now-I-don't-understand messy.

I admit, messy spirituality sounds...well...*unspiritual*.

Surely there are guidelines to follow, principles to live by, maps to show us where to go, and secrets we can uncover to find a spirituality that is clean and tidy.

I'm afraid not.

Spirituality is not a formula; it is not a test. It is a relationship. Spirituality is not about competency; it is about intimacy. Spirituality is not about perfection; it is about connection. The way of the spiritual life begins where we are *now* in the mess of our lives. Accepting the reality of our broken, flawed lives is the beginning of spirituality not because the spiritual life will remove our flaws but because we *let go* of seeking perfection and, instead, seek God, the one who is present in the tangledness of our lives. Spirituality is not about being fixed; it is about God's being present in the mess of our unfixedness.

Look at the Bible. Its pages overflow with messy people. The biblical writers did not edit out the flaws of its heroes. Like Noah, for example. Everyone thought he was crazy. He certainly was a little strange, but Noah was also courageous, a man of great faith and strong will. Against the backdrop of unrelenting ridicule, Noah built a huge ark in the middle of the desert because God told him it was going to rain. No one believed him, but the rains did come and the flood happened, and after the water receded, Noah triumphantly left the boat, *got drunk, and got naked.*[1]

What? *Drunk and naked?* I don't recall any of my Bible teachers or pastors talking about Noah's...uh...moment of indiscretion...er... weakness...um...failure. The Noah I've always heard about was fiercely faithful, irrepressibly independent, and relentlessly resolute. Noah was the model of great faith. Very few ever refer to Noah's losing battle with wine. Maybe being strong and faithful has its downside. Maybe for flood survivors life is more complicated than we would like to think, and maybe even Noah could have bouts of depression and loneliness.

Why should I be surprised? Turns out *all* of the biblical characters were a complex mix of strengths and weaknesses. David, Abraham, Lot, Saul, Solomon, Rahab, and Sarah were God-loving, courageous, brilliant, fearless, loyal, passionate, committed holy men and women who were also murderers, adulterers, and manic depressives. They were men and women who could be gentle, holy, defenders of the faith one minute, and insecure, mentally unstable, unbelieving, shrewd, lying, grudge-holding tyrants the next.

The New Testament characters weren't much better. Look who Jesus hung out with. Prostitutes, tax collectors, adulterers, mental cases, penniless riffraff, and losers of all kinds. His disciples were hardly models of saintliness. They were committed to Jesus, were ready to follow him anywhere (with one notable exception), but they were also troubled by infighting, always jockeying for position, suspicious of each other, accusatory, impulsive, selfish, lazy, and disloyal. Most of the time, they did not understand what Jesus was talking about, and when he died, they had no clue what to do next.

One very clear example of the messiness of the disciples took place in a tiny Samaritan village. On their way to Jerusalem, Jesus and the disciples stopped in this village for the evening. The Samaritans, however, weren't in a mood to cooperate. Most Jews didn't give Samaritans the time of day, so the Samaritans decided to return the favor by making it clear that Jesus and his disciples weren't welcome in their town. James and John (this would be the *beloved* disciple John) were furious, storming up to Jesus with the very undisciplelike question, "Lord, do you want us to call fire down from heaven to destroy them?"[2] Not exactly an example of mature, unmessy discipleship.

You might say Christianity has a tradition of messy spirituality. Messy prophets, messy kings, messy disciples, messy apostles. From God's people getting in one mess after another in the Old Testament to most of the New Testament's being written to straighten out messes in the church, the Bible presents a glorious story of a very messy faith.

Sounds like you and I are in good company.

Messy Spirituality unveils the myth of flawlessness and calls Christians everywhere to come out of hiding and stop pretending.

Messy Spirituality has the audacity to suggest that messiness is the workshop of authentic spirituality, the greenhouse of faith, the place where the real Jesus meets the real us.

Notorious Sinners

A few years ago, I was introduced to a group of uncouth Christians who call themselves "the Notorious Sinners." These are men from all walks of life who meet once a year to openly share their messy spirituality with each other. The title Notorious Sinners refers to the scandalous category of forgiven sinners whose reputations and ongoing flaws didn't seem to keep Jesus away. In fact, Jesus had a habit of collecting disreputables; he called them disciples. He still does. I like people who openly admit their notoriousness—people who unabashedly confess they are hopelessly flawed and hopelessly forgiven. Graciously, these men invited me to be a part of their group.

The Notorious Sinners meet yearly at spiritual-retreat centers, where from the moment we arrive, we find ourselves in trouble with the centers' leadership. We don't act like most contemplatives who come to spiritual-retreat centers—reserved, quiet, silently seeking the voice of God. We're a different kind of contemplative—earthy, boisterous, noisy, and rowdy, tromping around our souls seeking God, hanging out with a rambunctious Jesus who is looking for a good time in our hearts. A number of us smoke cigars, about half are recovering alcoholics, and a couple of the men could embarrass a sailor with their language. Two of the Notorious Sinners show up on their Harleys, complete with leather pants and leather jackets.

I admit I run with a rough crowd—Christians whose discipleship is blatantly real and carelessly passionate, characterized by a brazen godliness. Unafraid to admit their flaws, unintimidated by Christians who deny their own messiness, these guys sometimes look like pagans and other times look like Jesus. They are spiritual troublemakers, really, which is why they look like Jesus (who was always causing trouble himself). They are full of mischief, laughter, and boisterous behavior, which is why they look like pagans. Truly messy disciples. The Notorious Sinners are definitely a bizarre mix of the good, the bad, and the ugly, living a spirituality which defies simple definitions. Oh, and they are some of the most spiritual men I know.

Messy Spirituality is a description of the Christianity most of us live and that few of us admit. It is an attempt to break through the religious wall of secrecy and legitimize a faith which is unfinished, incomplete, and inexperienced. *Messy Spirituality* is a celebration of a discipleship which is under construction.

Messy Spirituality is the scandalous assertion that following Christ is anything but tidy and neat, balanced and orderly. Far from it. Spirituality is complex, complicated, and perplexing—the disorderly, sloppy, chaotic look of authentic faith in the real world.

Spirituality is anything but a straight line; it is a mixed-up, topsy-turvy, helter-skelter godliness that turns our lives into an upside-down toboggan ride full of unexpected turns, surprise bumps, and bone-shattering crashes. In other words, messy spirituality is the delirious consequence of a life ruined by a Jesus who will love us right into his arms.

The Scandal of Spirituality

Jesus is not repelled by us, no matter how messy we are, regardless of how incomplete we are. When we recognize that Jesus is not discouraged by our humanity, is not turned off by our messiness, and simply doggedly pursues us in the face of it all, what else can we do but give in to his outrageous, indiscriminate love?

Anne Lamott, a fellow messy Christian, describes perfectly what happens when Jesus pursues us. In her book *Traveling Mercies*, Anne recounts her conversion to Jesus. Things were not going well in her life: addicted to cocaine and alcohol, involved in an affair that produced a child whom she aborted, helplessly watching her best friend die of cancer. During this time, Anne visited a small church periodically. She would sit in the back to listen to the singing and then leave before the sermon. During the week of her abortion, she spiraled downward. Disgusted with herself, she drowned her sorrows in alcohol and drugs. She had been bleeding for many hours from the abortion and finally fell into bed, shaky and sad, smoked a cigarette, and turned off the light.

> After a while, as I lay there, I became aware of someone
> with me, hunkered down in the corner, and I just
> assumed it was my father, whose presence I had felt

over the years when I was frightened and alone. The feeling was so strong that I actually turned on the light for a moment to make sure no one was there—of course, there wasn't. But after a while, in the dark again, I knew beyond any doubt that it was Jesus. I felt him as surely as I feel my dog lying nearby as I write this.

And I was appalled...I thought about what everyone would think of me if I became a Christian, and it seemed an utterly impossible thing that simply could not be allowed to happen. I turned to the wall and said out loud, "I would rather die."

I felt him just sitting there on his haunches in the corner of my sleeping loft, watching me with patience and love, and I squinched my eyes shut, but that didn't help because that's not what I was seeing him with.

Finally I fell asleep, and in the morning, he was gone.

This experience spooked me badly, but I thought it was just an apparition, born of fear and self-loathing and booze and loss of blood. But then everywhere I went, I had the feeling that a little cat was following me, wanting me to reach down and pick it up, wanting me to open the door and let it in. But I knew what would happen: you let a cat in one time, give it a little milk, and then it stays forever...

And one week later, when I went back to church, I was so hungover that I couldn't stand up for the songs, and this time I stayed for the sermon, which I just thought was so ridiculous, like someone trying to convince me of the existence of extraterrestrials, but the last song was so deep and raw and pure that I could not escape. It was as if the people were singing in between the notes, weeping and joyful at the same time, and I felt like their voices or something was rocking me in its bosom, holding me like a scared kid, and I opened up to that feeling—and it washed over me.

> I began to cry and left before the benediction, and I
> raced home and felt the little cat running along at my
> heels, and I walked down the dock past dozens of
> potted flowers, under a sky as blue as one of God's
> own dreams, and I opened the door to my houseboat,
> and I stood there a minute, and then I hung my head
> and said,... "I quit." I took a long deep breath and said
> out loud, "All right. You can come in."
>
> So this was my beautiful moment of conversion.[3]

Anne Lamott is the most improbable candidate for spirituality
I could imagine, until I consider my own candidacy. Anne Lamott
seems hopelessly messed up until I remember the mess of my own
life. I recognize "the little cat running along" at her heels. He's the
same "cat" who's been hounding this messy follower of Christ all his
life. No matter how hard I've tried, I've never been able to shake him.
You won't be able to shake him either. So we might as well give up, as
Anne did, and let "the cat" in. Then we can decide what we're going to
do with the not-so-little Jesus who, running wild in our hearts, will
wreak havoc in our souls, transforming our messy humanity into a
messy spirituality.

1.   Genesis 9:20–28.

2.   Luke 9:51–56.

3.   Anne Lamott, *Traveling Mercies: Some Thoughts on Faith* (New York:
     Pantheon, 1999), 49–50.

MESSY SPIRITUALITY:

The Place Where Our Messiness and Jesus Meet

Mike Yaconelli

When we sin and mess up our lives, we find
that God doesn't go off and leave us—he enters
into our trouble and saves us.
EUGENE PETERSON, A LONG OBEDIENCE IN THE SAME DIRECTION

I myself walked up to the Ragman. I told him my
name with shame, for I was a sorry figure next to him.
Then I took off all my clothes in that place, and I said to
him with a dear yearning in my voice: "Dress me."
He dressed me, my Lord, he put new rags on me,
and I am a wonder beside him.
WALTER WANGERIN, RAGMAN AND OTHER CRIES OF FAITH

Our churches are filled with people who outwardly
look contented and at peace but inwardly are crying
out for someone to love them...just as they are—confused,
frustrated, often frightened, guilty, and often unable to
communicate even within their own families. But the other
people in the church look so happy and contented
that one seldom has the courage to admit his own
deep needs before such a self-sufficient group as
the average church meeting appears to be.
KEITH MILLER

He who thinks that he is finished is finished. How true.
Those who think that they have arrived, have lost their way.
Those who think they have reached their goal, have missed it.
Those who think they are saints, are demons.
HENRI NOUWEN, THE GENESEE DIARY

One of my favorite *Peanuts* cartoons starts with Lucy at her five-cent psychology booth, where Charlie Brown has stopped for advice about life.

"Life is like a deck chair, Charlie," she says. "On the cruise ship of life, some people place their deck chair at the rear of the ship so they can see where they've been. Others place their deck chair at the front of the ship so they can see where they're going."

The good "doctor" looks at her puzzled client and asks, "Which way is your deck chair facing?"

Without hesitating, Charlie replies glumly, "I can't even get my deck chair unfolded."

Charlie and I are soul mates.

Everywhere I look on the cruise ship of Christianity, I see crews of instructors, teachers, experts, and gurus eager to explain God's plan for the placement of my deck chair, but I still can't even unfold it. No wonder, when I peruse the titles in a Christian bookstore, I feel like I am the only klutz in the kingdom of God, a spiritual nincompoop lost in a shipful of brilliant biblical thinkers, an ungodly midget in a world of spiritual giants. When I compare my life with the experts', I feel sloppy, unkempt, and messy in the midst of immaculately dressed saints...*and I'm a minister.* Maybe that's why God allowed me to pastor a church "for people who don't like to go to church." When your "pastor" was kicked out of two Bible colleges, maybe it's easier for people not to be intimidated by some ideal of spirituality.

Many of those who attend our church have always wanted to go to church, wanted to know God better, longed for a better relationship with Jesus, but more often than not, they would end up at a church where they were made to feel as if the "mess" of their lives disqualified them from the possibility of an authentic spiritual life. Let me describe for you the "messy" lives of those who might be sitting in our church on any given Sunday.

Rene: after thirty years of marriage, her husband left her for a younger woman, right after Rene was diagnosed with lung cancer. Devastated and alone, she is slowly trying to follow Jesus in the wreckage of her situation. She was made to feel guilty by her former church because her marriage fell apart. Her faith didn't heal the cancer, her children are not in a good place, and she is having bouts of depression (which "spiritual" Christians shouldn't have, according to her "spiritual" friends), wondering what happened to the good life God was supposed to provide her with.

Darrell: struggling with a long history of abuse and drugs, he usually finds his way to church after a night of drinking. Darrell sits in the last row in a seat close to the door because he doesn't want people to see his swollen face, his red eyes, his unshaven beard. He's ashamed that he cannot tame his drinking problem. He has been told at other churches that if he were totally committed to living a spiritual life, drinking wouldn't be a problem. Trying doesn't count, his church friends have said to him.

Carol: divorced, alone. She went through hell last year dealing with a dying father who required too much of her time because other family members refused to do their part. Now in the aftermath she is left with guilt and anger and the struggle to understand what spirituality looks like in the midst of her ragged and weary day-to-day life. She was told by many of her friends in her previous church that spiritual people don't get divorces, get angry, feel guilty, or resent their families.

Gary and Linda, Carl and Doreen: two of many couples who are facing midlife crises, empty nest syndromes, and the haunting question, "Is this all there is?" These couples are besieged with doubts about Christianity. In their previous church experiences, they were reminded repeatedly that spiritual people don't have midlife crises, nor are they haunted by doubts and fears, because Jesus is the answer to all their questions and insecurities.

Lillian, Regina, Don, and Barbara: older members of our church whose spouses have died. They have decided they are too old to start a new relationship, they feel patronized but not befriended, and they wonder if their last years will be lived out alone.

The list could go on and on. Sprinkled throughout our congregation are good people who have been paralyzed by feelings of inadequacy and unworthiness, insecurity and self-doubt, insignificance and guilt, which are what cripples most of us who are trying to follow Christ.

What Does Messy Spirituality Look Like?

This may sound shocking to some, but spirituality is a home for those who don't have life figured out, who don't know the Bible as well as they could, and who don't have their spiritual lives all together —*the rest of us* who thought there wasn't a "rest of us," Christians who are *trying to follow Jesus the best we can.*

A couple of years ago, my wife and I sat across the table from a woman we highly respect, a deeply spiritual lady who had profoundly impacted our lives. This woman spent most of her life resisting the noise and activity of the world to seek God in silence and solitude. She had spent hundreds of weeks in silent retreat. This was a woman so saturated with her faith, you could almost smell God when she came into the room.

We were talking about prayer. "It's embarrassing to be sitting with you," I blurted. "You spend days, weeks, even months in prayer. I'm lucky if I spend ten minutes. Compared to you, I'm not very spiritual, I'm afraid."

Her eyes, flashing with anger, caught mine, and she fired back, "Oh, Mike, knock it off. First of all, you don't spend every day with me. You don't know me at all. You are comparing what you know about yourself to what you don't know about me. Secondly, I battle depression daily, and it has won during several periods of my life. I never told you about it. I don't have a family; I like to be alone and silent. Trust me, I am just as 'unspiritual' as you are."

Then she said gently, "You think about God all the time, right?"

"Well, sort of," I said.

"Thinking about God is being with God. Being with God is spirituality. Thinking about God is praying. So shut up with this guilt stuff; you have been praying most of your life! You are a spiritual person!"

What? I've been praying most of my life? What was she talking about? It never occurred to me that Paul's "pray without ceasing" might actually be possible. It never occurred to me that praying could include thinking, that praying could be done with my *eyes open*, that praying could be done standing, sitting, driving, dancing, skiing, lying down, jogging, working. How could anyone accuse *me* of praying all the time when I didn't pray all the time...unless my friend was right, unless I was praying without ceasing?

How could anyone accuse me of being spiritual unless spirituality comes in unlimited shapes and sizes, unless spirituality looks like whatever you and I look like when we're thinking about Jesus, when we are trying to find Jesus, when we are trying to figure out what real Christianity looks like in the real world?

Spirituality looks like whatever you and I look like when we're thinking about Jesus, when we are trying to find Jesus, when we are trying to figure out what real Christianity looks like in the real world.

Unpretending

There is no room for pretending in the spiritual life. Unfortunately, in many religious circles, there exists an unwritten rule. Pretend. Act like God is in control when you don't believe he is. Give the impression everything is okay in your life when it's not. Pretend you believe when you doubt; hide your imperfections; maintain the image of a perfect marriage with healthy and well-adjusted children when your family is like any other normal dysfunctional family. And whatever you do, don't admit that you sin.

Practically, pretending is efficient, uncomplicated, and quick. Answering "Fine" to the question "How are you doing?" is much easier and quicker than saying, "Not very well, thank you; my back is bothering me, my teenage children are disappointing me, I'm unhappy with my body, my husband never speaks to me, and I'm wondering if Christianity is true." Honesty requires a huge investment of time and energy from the person asking the question (who would then wish they'd never asked).

Pretending is the grease of modern nonrelationships. Pretending perpetuates the illusion of relationships by connecting us on the basis of who we aren't. People who pretend have pretend relationships. But being real is a synonym for messy spirituality, because when we are real, our messiness is there for everyone to see.

Some people consider the use of words like *messy spirituality* rude and audacious. "How dare you suggest that people are messy? What are you proposing? Are you suggesting that sin is okay, that we should condone less than a 100 percent effort to serve God? You are too negative. It's not helpful to emphasize our flaws."

But the truth is, we *are* a mess. None of us is who we appear to be. We all have secrets. We all have issues. We all struggle from time to time. No one is perfect. Not one. (I have just paraphrased Romans 3:10.) The essence of messy spirituality is the refusal to pretend, to lie, or to allow others to believe we are something we are not. Unfortunately, people can handle the most difficult issues more easily than they can handle the lack of pretending.

When you and I stop pretending, we expose the pretending of everyone else. The bubble of the perfect Christian life is burst, and we all must face the reality of our brokenness.

When my eighteen-month-old daughter was diagnosed with cancer, I was unprepared for the pretending of my Christian friends. Within hours of the news getting out, I was inundated with statements like, "I'm sure God is doing this for a reason. God can heal your daughter if you just have faith. Even if she dies, she will be better off." I remember answering these people, "I hope God is *not* doing this. I don't believe God promises to heal my daughter. Certainly dying is never better than living, otherwise we should all commit suicide." You can imagine the responses of those around me. They wrote off my statements to shock, bitterness, cynicism, and lack of faith. But I *wasn't* bitter; I *wasn't* cynical. I was *telling the truth*. I could not, *would not* pretend anymore.

Was I confused about exactly where God was? Of course. Did I have serious questions about my faith? Yes. Was I desperate, depressed, angry, resentful? Yes, I was all those things. I only wish others could have given me the space to be honest and that they could have been honest too. I look back now, twenty-nine years later, and I realize these people were confused and afraid themselves. If they could get me to agree with them, then they would no longer be afraid. But I couldn't do it. They were forced to deal with the reality of an eighteen-month-old baby who could have died from a terrible disease. (She is very much alive, by the way.) Even today, if you were to ask me why my daughter lived, I would have only one answer: "I don't know." I watched a lot of children Lisa's age die during the same period that she was ill, and for the life of me, I don't know where God was. I cannot pretend the mystery of God away.

Sermons are not always amazing masterpieces of truth, wit, and insight. Sometimes the sermon just doesn't work, doesn't connect. It just lies there in a pile while the minister desperately tries to resuscitate it. I was having one of those Sundays. My sermon was just not connecting, people were bored, looking at their watches, and at one point, almost in unison, a majority of the congregation looked back at the clock on the wall. I had no choice; I had to admit the truth.

"I...uh...realize I've gone a little long today. Sorry, but I have just one more point I'd like to make."

Sadie, lovely honest Sadie, threw her hands to her face and yelled, "Oooh nooo!" causing the rest of the congregation to laugh...and then applaud. Most people were trying to stifle what they were really feeling, but not Sadie. Luckily her condition of Down's syndrome doesn't allow her to understand pretending, so she said not only what she thought but what everyone else thought as well.

The sermon was over. Thank God...and thank Sadie.

Spiritual people tell the truth.

Unfinishedness

Spiritual people also admit their unfinishedness. Unfinished means incomplete, imperfect, in process, in progress, under construction. Spiritual describes someone who is incomplete, imperfectly living their life for God. The construction site of our souls exposes our flaws, the rough-hewn, not-finished faith clearly visible in our hearts. When we seek God, Jesus begins to take shape in our lives. He *begins* a good work in us, he *starts* changing us, but the finishing process is a more-than-a-lifetime process. The work of God in our lives *will never be finished* until we meet Jesus face to face. The author of Hebrews wrote, "Let us fix our eyes on Jesus, the author and perfecter [or finisher] of our faith."[1] Spirituality isn't about being finished and perfect; spirituality is about trusting God in our unfinishedness.

I'll never forget the day Eric, a recovering alcoholic, stood up in our church during announcements. Eric's lifelong battle with alcohol had been mostly unsuccessful. He had been in and out of jail, and his drinking was taking its toll on his marriage.

"I need prayer," he said. "My wife has given me an ultimatum— drinking or her. She's asked me to decide today, and I just wanted to tell you all that I have decided..."

A long awkward pause ensued, and every person in the church was on the edge of their seat with their face turned toward him, encouraging him, pleading with him to make the right decision. You could have heard a pin drop.

Finally, he stumbled on, tears in his eyes. "I've decided to choose my wife!"

Applause and cheering broke out. No one said it, but you could hear it anyway: "Good answer! Good answer!" Eric was not afraid to tell the truth; he was not afraid to reveal to all of us how difficult it was to give up alcohol, even for his wife. Eric is a spiritual man. Troubled? Yes. Weak? Yes. Unfinished? Absolutely! But Eric told the truth and admitted that his desire for drinking was conflicting with his desire to stay married. Eric refused to pretend life is clean and neat, and he knew he had to tell us the way things were, not the way we wished they were.

Jesus understood unfinishedness very well, which is why he was comfortable leaving eleven unfinished disciples. When he died, the disciples were confused, depressed, afraid, and doubtful. They faced a lifetime of finishing, just like you and me. Messy spirituality not only reminds us we will always be a work in progress; it also reminds us that the unfinished life is a lot more spiritual than we imagined.

Incompetence

Messy spirituality describes our godly incompetence. No one does holy living very well. Spirituality is the humiliating recognition that I don't know how to pray well. I don't understand God's Word or know how to navigate it properly, and I don't know how to competently live out my commitment to Christ. Messy spirituality affirms our spiritual clumsiness.

I grew up in a church where dancing was frowned upon. As a result, four decades later, I still can't dance. Even worship dancing causes my heart to race because I am desperately afraid of anyone seeing my stiff, awkward attempts to make my body move. Because I am a lousy dancer, I avoid any experience in which dancing is a possibility.

When it comes to the spiritual life, I am amazed how many of us don't know how to dance. We stand before God, the music starts playing, and we are embarrassed by our incompetence. The church has communicated that competence is one of the fruits of the Spirit and that, therefore, spiritual people are supposed to live faith competently. So many people are afraid of embracing the spiritual life because of the possibility they might say or do the incompetent thing.

One Sunday morning, Gary, a new Christian in our church, offered to read the Scripture for the day, which was the second chapter of Acts. During the worship service, I could see him in the front row, Bible in hand, checking the bulletin to make sure he wouldn't miss his moment. When the time came, Gary stood in front of the congregation and thumbed through his Bible, searching for the book of Acts...and searching...and searching. Finally, after two awkward minutes, he turned around and said sheepishly, "Uh, I can find the first book of Acts, but where is the second book of Acts?" Everyone laughed and someone graciously led him to the second *chapter* of the only book of Acts in the Bible. Luckily, our church is a church which expects incompetence.

Jesus responds to desire. Which is why he responded to people who interrupted him, yelled at him, touched him, screamed obscenities at him, barged in on him, crashed through ceilings to get to him. *Jesus cares more about desire than about competence.*

My hunch is most of you reading this book feel incompetent *and* you can't let go of Jesus. Jesus sees right through your incompetence into a heart longing for him.

It was time for the Scripture reading and a girl shuffled toward the front of the church. What a moment for Connie. She had finally mustered enough courage to ask the pastor if she could read the Scripture. Without hesitation, he said yes. For years Connie had stifled her desire to serve in the church because of her "incompetencies." Reading was extremely difficult for her, and Connie had a terrible time enunciating clearly. But she had been in this church many years, and she was beginning to understand the grace of God. Jesus didn't die just for our sins; he died so people who couldn't read or speak could read and speak. Now she could serve the Jesus she loved so much. Now she could express her desire for God in a tangible way.

Connie's steps were labored as she made her way to the front; one leg was shorter than the other, causing her body to teeter from side to side. Finally, she was standing up front, looking at the congregation with pride and joy.

The congregation was silent. Too silent.

The screaming silence was covering up the congregation's discomfort. Clearly, most of them were trying to understand what Connie was doing, and they were trying not to notice her many incompetencies. Her eyes were too close together, and her head twisted back and forth at odd angles while her face wrenched from one grimace to another.

Connie began to read, and stammering, stuttering, she stumbled proudly through the passage in a long sequence of untranslatable sounds, garbled sentences, long tortuous pauses, and jumbled phrases. Finally, the reading was over, and the congregation was exhausted.

Connie didn't notice the exhaustion. She was ecstatic. Her face seemed no longer distorted, only full of joy. Her cheeks were flush with pride; her eyes were sparkling with the joy of accomplishment; her heart was warm with knowing she had *served* the congregation, participated in her faith. Yes, she would remember this day for a long time. How wonderful it was, she thought, to no longer be a *spectator* in church; she *was* the church this morning!

Thank God her mental capacities were limited. Thank God she was not able to discern the faces of the congregation or she would have crumbled in despair. Thank God she wasn't able to sense what people were really thinking.

Almost everyone in the congregation was thinking, *This is an outrage!* I know this is what they were thinking, because the senior pastor, my father, was ordered to attend an emergency board meeting after the service.

"How did this happen?" they demanded to know. "What were you thinking?"

"Connie wanted to read the Scripture," he replied softly.

"Well, let her stand at the door and pass out bulletins, or help in the mailroom, but don't have her read! The girl can't read or speak. Her reading took ten minutes! The church," they said, "is not a place for incompetence."

My father believes, as I do, that the church is the place where the incompetent, the unfinished, and even the unhealthy are welcome. I believe Jesus agrees.

From Messy Spirituality *by Mike Yaconelli*

Desperateness

Christianity is not for people who think religion is a pleasant distraction, a nice alternative, or a positive influence. Messy spirituality is a good term for the place where desperation meets Jesus. More often than not, in Jesus' day, desperate people who tried to get to Jesus were surrounded by religious people who either ignored or rejected those who were seeking to have their hunger for God filled. Sadly, not much has changed over the years.

Desperate people don't do well in churches. They don't fit, and they don't cooperate in the furthering of their starvation. "Church people" often label "desperate people" as strange and unbalanced. But when desperate people get a taste of God, they can't stay away from him, no matter what everyone around them thinks.

Desperate is a strong word. That's why I like it. People who are desperate are rude, frantic, and reckless. Desperate people are explosive, focused, and uncompromising in their desire to get what they want. Someone who is desperate will crash through the veil of niceness. The New Testament is filled with desperate people, people who barged into private dinners, screamed at Jesus until they had his attention, or destroyed the roof of someone's house to get to him. People who are desperate for spirituality very seldom worry about the mess they make on their way to be with Jesus.

Barbara Brown Taylor pastored a downtown church for many years. The sanctuary was open during the day, but unfortunately, because of the kind of world we live in, a closed-circuit camera was installed to monitor what went on inside. The receptionist of the church checked the monitor throughout the day.

One day during a staff meeting, the receptionist interrupted to report, "There's a man lying face down on the altar steps. I wouldn't bother you, but he's been there for hours. Every now and then he stands up, raises his arms toward the altar, and lies down again." One of the staff went out to speak to the man, to find out if he was okay, and reported, "He says he's praying." They decided to leave the man alone. But he returned every day, lying on the altar steps. His clothes were worn and dirty; his hair was in knots. The staff instructed the sexton and the altar guild not to disturb the man and to work around him.

Finally, it was Sunday, and as Barbara entered the sanctuary for the early service, she saw the man blocking her path to the altar. She was afraid. What if he was crazy? She approached him cautiously, noticing how dirty he was, how emaciated he was from lack of food. She explained to him that a service was to begin in a few minutes and he would have to leave. He lifted his forehead from the floor and, speaking with a heavy Haitian accent, said, "That's okay."

Barbara describes what happened after he left:

> The eight o'clock service began on time. The faithful
> took their places and I took mine. We read our parts
> well. We spoke when we were supposed to speak
> and were silent when we were supposed to be silent.
> We offered up our symbolic gifts, we performed our
> bounden duty and service, and there was nothing
> wrong with what we did, nothing at all. We were good
> servants, careful and contrite sinners who had come for
> our ritual cleansing, but one of us was missing. He had
> risen and gone his way, but the place where he lay on
> his face for hours—making a spectacle of himself—
> seemed all at once so full of heat and light that I
> stepped around it on my way out, chastened if only
> for that moment by the call to a love so excessive,
> so disturbing, so beyond the call to obedience that it
> made me want to leave all my good works behind.[2]

I wish the man had been invited to stay for the worship service. Maybe Barbara did invite him and he declined. Regardless, I believe Jesus would have asked him to stay. In any case, a desperate man, covered with dirt and hair clotted from days of abuse, filled a sanctuary with the spectacle of God's presence.

When the Unqualified Are Qualified

Walking by a pet shop on his way to school, a young boy stopped and stared through the window. Inside were four black puppies playing together. After school he ran home and pleaded with his mother to let him have one of the puppies. "I'll take care of it, Mom, I will. If you can just give me an advance on my allowance, I'll have enough money to buy one with my own money. Please, Mom, please."

The mother, knowing full well the complications having a new puppy would bring to a busy household, could not resist her son. "Okay, you can get the puppy, but I will expect you to take care of it."

"Yes, Mom, I will." Filled with excitement, the little boy ran to the pet shop to buy his new puppy.

After determining that the boy had enough money, the pet shop owner brought him to the window to choose his puppy. After a few minutes, the young boy said, "Um...I'll take the little one in the corner."

"Oh no," said the shop owner, "not that one; he's crippled. Notice how he just sits there; something is wrong with one of his legs, so he can't run and play like the rest of the puppies. Choose another one."

Without saying a word, the boy reached down, lifted his pant leg to expose a chrome leg brace to the owner.

"No," he said firmly, "I think I'll take the puppy in the corner."[3]

It turned out that what disqualified the puppy from being chosen by others is what most qualified him to be chosen by the little boy.

It's amazing how few of us believe in the unqualified grace of God. Oh, yes, God loves us, as long as we're clean and whole and fixed. But it turns out that what disqualifies you and me from "spirituality"—the mess of our lives and our crippledness—is what most qualifies us to be chosen by Jesus.

The Myth of Fixing Ourselves

For a period of time, we were lucky enough to have a housekeeper. She would come in once a week to dust, vacuum, and clean every little out-of-the-way corner of our house. I dreaded the day she came, because my wife and I would spend all morning *cleaning the house for the housekeeper!* We didn't want the house to be dirty, or what would the housekeeper think?!

We act the same way with God. We talk our way out of the spiritual life by refusing to come to God as we are. Instead, we decide to wait until we are ready to come to God as we aren't. We decide that the way we lived yesterday, last week, or last year makes us "damaged goods" and that until we start living "right," we're not "God material." Some of us actually believe that until we choose the correct way to live, we aren't chooseable, that until we clean up the mess, Jesus won't have anything to do with us. The opposite is true. *Until we admit we are a mess*, Jesus won't have anything to do with us. Once we admit how unlovely we are, how unattractive we are, how lost we are, Jesus shows up unexpectedly. According to the New Testament, Jesus is attracted to the unattractive. He prefers the lost ones over the found ones, the losers over the winners, the broken instead of the whole, the messy instead the unmessy, the crippled instead of the noncrippled.

Dancing the Undanceable

Lost in my thoughts, I was sitting in a hotel ballroom with fifteen hundred college students participating in a weekend faith conference. On the last day of the conference, with school starting the following Monday, the students made it clear they wanted to prolong the conference as long as possible. They wanted to party, to dance the afternoon away, to celebrate the Lord of the dance—to resist going back into the busyness and demands of college life. The morning general session turned into a spontaneous celebration. Young men and women raised their hands, stood on chairs, shouted, cried, and laughed, and then suddenly a conga line broke out. Within seconds, hundreds of college students were weaving in and out of the room in long, raucous lines praising their God.

An older man with cerebral palsy sat in a motorized wheelchair, watching everyone else party. (He wasn't a college student. Technically he wasn't even supposed to be at the conference.) I was seated next to him, watching the students celebrate, when suddenly the wheelchair lunged into the celebration. The man's arms waved, his chair careened around the room with a jerky, captivating motion, his mouth struggled open and shut making incomprehensible sounds. Somehow a man who couldn't dance had become part of the graceful dancing of the crowd. Without warning, his motorized wheelchair lurched to the base of the stage, racing back and forth through a series of figure eights, twirls, and circles. He was laughing, lost in the joy of the Lord. His joy had taken a cold, ugly piece of motorized machinery and transformed it into an extension of his unconfined worship. He and his wheelchair had become one, a dancing, living thing. This man with a crippled body found a way to dance the undanceable.

I envy him. I want my crippled soul to escape the cold and sterile spirituality of a religion where only the perfect nondisabled get in. I want to lurch forward to Jesus, where the unwelcome receive welcome and the unqualified get qualified. I want to hear Jesus tell me I can dance when everyone else says I can't. I want to hear Jesus walk over and whisper to this handicapped, messy Christian, "Do you want to dance?"

1.   Hebrews 12:2.
2.   Barbara Brown Taylor, *The Preaching Life* (Boston: Cowley, 1993), 110–12.
3.   Ron Lee Davis, *A Forgiving God in an Unforgiving World* (Eugene, Ore.: Harvest House, 1984), 63.

THE MAN WHO WOULDN'T LISTEN

Jim Cymbala

The Search

Throughout history mankind has been searching for one thing or another: for knowledge, for new lands, for freedom from religious and political persecution, and for valuable resources such as gold, diamonds, and oil. People have searched for new pleasures, the perfect mate, and peace in the midst of fighting and carnage. There has also been an age-old quest for inner peace and for understanding the real reason for our existence.

Out of this quest comes one of the greatest searches: the one to know and experience God. Inside the human heart is an undeniable, spiritual instinct to commune with its Creator. We can deny, ignore, or bury that instinct under an avalanche of material things, but the fact that we were created to enjoy God and to worship him forever is etched upon our souls.

Countless people have chronicled their search for the Almighty. Testimonies abound of the life-changing nature of an encounter with God, who sent his Son into the world so that men and women "may have life, and have it to the full" (John 10:10). But as interesting as man's quest for God is, it merely points to a far more significant search that I want us to consider in this book.

That search was revealed long ago when God sent a prophet to deliver a message to King Asa in Jerusalem. Although the Lord was correcting Asa for his lack of faith and devotion, the prophetic word contained a declaration that God himself was involved in a unique search! In describing God's love and desire to bless his people, the prophet declared a truth that is staggering in its implications: "For the eyes of the Lord move to and fro throughout the earth that He may strongly support those whose heart is completely His" (2 Chronicles 16:9 NASB). Since God is unchanging, what was true during King Asa's day applies to us in the twenty-first century.

God is on a search. He is not looking for such things as knowledge or precious stones—after all, he knows everything and owns the world and everything in it. Although we rarely think about this or hear it preached, the Creator of all things is looking throughout the whole earth for a certain kind of heart. He is searching for a human heart that will allow him to show how marvelously he can strengthen, help, and bless someone's life.

Notice that God isn't seeking someone with a high IQ or multiple talents. Nor is he seeking the clever speaker or the person of influence. He revealed where his true interest lies when he sent the prophet Samuel to anoint the future king of Israel. God said, "Do not consider his appearance or his height...The Lord does not look at the things man looks at. Man looks at the outward appearance, but the Lord *looks at the heart*" (1 Samuel 16:7).

What made David special was his heart, and that principle has never changed. All the great men and women of Scripture had *great hearts* that permitted God's grace to flow through them and bring blessings to others. This truth was well understood by David, the young man whom God elevated to the throne. Before he died, David charged his son Solomon, "And you, my son Solomon, acknowledge the God of your father, and serve him with *wholehearted* devotion and with a willing mind, *for the Lord searches every heart* and understands every motive behind the thoughts" (1 Chronicles 28:9). It is what God sees behind the façade and outward behavior that determines the extent of his blessing. So King David wanted his son to pay very careful attention to his heart.

In the New Testament we read how Jesus saw through the outward shows of religion and affirmed the importance of a "right" heart when he condemned the hypocrisy of the Pharisees: "You are the ones who justify yourselves in the eyes of men, but *God knows your hearts*" (Luke 16:15). Jesus always looked into the heart, and there he found the real person.

Christianity is by necessity a religion of the heart because only out of the heart comes "the wellspring of life" (Proverbs 4:23). God calls people to turn to him with their *whole hearts*. Salvation is received when we believe *in our hearts* that God raised Jesus from the dead

(Romans 10:9). When Scripture bids us to pray, it asks us to *pour out our hearts* to the Lord (Psalm 62:8). Modern preaching puts an overwhelming emphasis on works and external forms of worship, but a real spiritual revival must always begin in the heart.

Notice the kind of heart to which God is drawn, as seen in Samuel's words to King Saul: "The Lord has sought out a man *after his own heart* and appointed him leader of his people" (1 Samuel 13:14). God's search for a king ended when he found obscure David and his very special heart. But what does it mean to have a special heart, "a heart after God"?

This is a most important subject for us to consider because it speaks to who we really are and to what extent God can use us for his glory. A heart out of tune, out of sync with God's heart, will produce a life of spiritual barrenness and missed opportunities. But as we ask the Lord to bring our hearts into harmony with and submission to his, we will find the secret of his blessings that has remained the same throughout all generations.

The Man Who Wouldn't Listen

A Sunday night service I will never forget started an unusual series of events I never could have imagined.

We were prepared to serve Communion to the congregation, and I was looking forward to preaching from the Word of God. In addition, a young couple—gospel singers from Nashville—were prepared to sing for us that night. But none of that ever happened. While we were singing praise songs to the Lord, an extended time of free-flowing worship began. As people poured out their adoration to God, an awesome sense of his presence filled the auditorium. All of us were overwhelmed as rivers of deeper and deeper praise ascended from our hearts to the Lord. All sense of time seemed to disappear as we became lost in God's presence. Nothing seemed to matter except worshiping "the Lamb at the center of the throne" (Revelation 7:17), the One who is worthy to be praised forever. It seemed as if wave after wave of God's glory rolled over us as we stood, sat, and knelt before him.

As I looked out over the congregation from the platform, I realized that God was doing a special work among us by his Spirit. A kind of divine surgery was going on as worship and praise mingled with petitions and intercessions. Conviction of sin was very strong, which always happens when the Spirit of God manifests his holy presence among his people. To stop or hinder what was going on seemed like a terrible grieving of the Spirit, so I never even took an offering that evening. The bills would wait. I just could not interrupt the wonderful ways in which the Lord was working in people's lives. The service ended hours later, and people were still kneeling or sitting quietly before the Lord when I finally left the auditorium.

Carol and I arrived home late. We were physically exhausted from a long day of ministering, but our hearts still basked in the afterglow of our time with the Lord. When I came out of the bathroom, Carol was already in bed and had turned on the television. We often watched the national broadcast of one of America's foremost televangelists late on Sunday nights. The program was usually a tape of one of his crusade meetings, and that night was no exception. The televangelist was already preaching his sermon when I began watching from the bathroom doorway.

During the previous months, we had been saddened by the increasingly shrill and harsh spirit of this man's preaching. Instead of carefully and humbly handling God's Word, his preaching was dominated by bombast and denunciations of sinners high and low. But we were not prepared for what he said that night.

As he discussed social evils contaminating America, he referred to a recent child molestation case featured prominently in the news. "I'll tell you what needs to be done with a person like that," he roared as he paced back and forth on the stage. "If I had my way, he'd be lined up and they would empty a shotgun into his chest!" Suddenly the crowd exploded; people leaped to their feet with a thunderous applause and shouted, "Amen."

My wife groaned, "O God, help us!" I was stunned, frozen where I stood. The spiritual shock of the evangelist's comments went deep. Our hearts were still tender from the hours we had just spent in the presence of the God who is *love*. Now we watched as more than fifteen thousand Christians cheered for the shooting of another human being whom God created! *No matter how awful this man's sin might have been,* I thought, *this is not what Jesus is about.* I had attended all kinds of church services in my life, but I had never experienced anything like this. The thought of the pulpit and a congregation being perverted like this absolutely took my breath away. The anger, venom, and vengeance on the screen before us were worlds apart from the Spirit of Jesus who prayed for those who were crucifying him.

The next thing I remember, Carol began sobbing and saying, "Please, Jim, turn it off. I can't watch anymore." I did as she asked and felt my tears welling up. *Is this what viewers around America need to hear?* I thought. *With all the problems around us, how can this be the good news Jesus told us to spread?*

"Someone has to talk to him, Jim, before it's too late," Carol blurted out as I began turning out the lights. "Something is really wrong in his spirit, and he will hurt the cause of the gospel before it's all over."

"I know," I said. I had the same ominous feeling as my wife, but it seemed there was little we could do.

"Can't you talk to your friend who knows him pretty well?" Carol asked. "Maybe he can counsel or warn him before it's too late."

I lay in bed that night praying that somehow God would stop this brother in Christ from pursuing what seemed to be a self-destructive course. Carol and I talked about the situation during the next week, but I didn't feel right about approaching my friend and asking him to intervene with someone of world renown whom I had never even met.

Eight days later, Carol and I again talked about the televangelist. Was there anything we could do for him—anything God wanted us to do?

Suddenly I felt a strong, distinct prompting to call my friend. He had a national ministry as well, and I knew he had spoken several times at the televangelist's school. I quickly picked up the phone and dialed his home. He answered, and after brief greetings I nervously got to the point of my call. "I really don't know how to say this, brother, and I sure don't want to put pressure on our friendship, but Carol and I are really troubled about something."

I quickly summarized our special Sunday night service and the spiritual pain we had felt upon hearing the televangelist's raw remarks.

I told my friend how deeply this had affected us and that we just couldn't put it aside. But the phone seemed to go dead on the other end as I rambled on. "Are you still there, brother?" I asked.

After a brief pause, he slowly and emotionally replied, "Go on, Jim."

"Well, that's really it. We're aware that you know him pretty well, and maybe there's something God would have you do. Somebody has to do something, or we feel he's going to self-destruct. Do you know what I mean?"

Again, there was a strange silence. I was almost sure I could hear quiet sobbing on the other end of the line. "Hey, maybe I'm calling at a bad time," I added nervously. "Maybe I shouldn't even be bothering you with stuff like this."

"Jim, I'm glad you called," my friend said. "God meant for us to talk right now."

He then told me that just ten days earlier he and his wife had visited the televangelist's school. My friend had gone there to preach and was alarmed by what he had seen and discerned. The pace and pressure were so overwhelming, the financial crush so phenomenal, and the broadcasting and crusade schedule so demanding that the televangelist had no time for spiritual priorities. My friend saw him becoming spiritually shallow. Careful Bible study, time alone with the Lord, time alone with his wife—these essentials were being overrun by a monstrous empire that demanded all of his time and energy. My friend returned home with a broken heart and warning signals sounding inside him.

But that wasn't all. While in prayer a few nights before my call, my friend felt God's Spirit come upon him. The Lord seemed to give him a prophetic word of warning for the televangelist. With godly fear and trembling, he wrote it out in a letter. The main thrust of the letter was, "Shut it down. God wants you to shut it all down no matter what the cost may be. Get back to prayer, the Word, your family—get back to God. Don't worry about the supposed cost of shutting everything down, because the cost will be greater if you don't go back to your spiritual roots of communion with God."

My friend said he had prepared the letter for mailing but told his secretary not to send it until he gave the word. He wanted to be sure the Spirit of God was leading him because he knew that the letter could cost him his friendship with the televangelist. As my friend prayed that night in his study, he asked God to give him a sign—some confirmation that sending the letter of warning was of the Lord. That's when the phone rang. There I was on the other end, bringing up the very same subject!

The letter was sent the next day, but the response was not encouraging. My friend was told that his discernment and "word from the Lord" were way off base. The televangelist could never think of "shutting it all down" because too much was at stake—too many cities and countries to reach, too many television contracts signed, too many crusades planned, too much money coming in daily—to think that God could ever say something as radical as "shut it all down!"

The televangelist never listened to our mutual friend whom God used to warn him of the perils ahead. Soon the day came when he probably wished he had listened, wished he had shut it all down. But by then it was too late. By then his name and picture were known around the world as a symbol of scandal and shame. The spiritual cancer that had been growing for a long time had finally claimed its victim. All the tears and public apologies came too late to stop his life from careening out of control. In the end, it was *all* shut down—the empire, the international television ministry, the massive crusades. It became part of one of the saddest religious stories of the twentieth century.

I was much younger then as I watched the story unfold before me. I knew of at least one hidden episode of God's efforts to save the televangelist before his nasty fall. God is faithful, and God is love. The problem was, God was speaking but nobody was listening.

The problem was, God was speaking but nobody was listening.

From beginning to end, the Word of God greatly emphasizes the need to listen. We all make mistakes, fail to do God's will perfectly, and even rebel against his commands. But when we refuse to listen to his voice of correction and direction, things can quickly reach critical mass.

I remember how true this was on the playgrounds of Brooklyn where I played as a kid. Basketball was my thing; I devoted myself to the game. When I began playing on the varsity team at Erasmus Hall High School—a school with a great basketball tradition—I noticed something odd right away. The guys I knew from the park could play really well, but they never made the team, which meant that receiving a college athletic scholarship was out of the question. Many of these talented guys had one main problem: they wouldn't listen. No coach was going to change anything about their game. No, sir! No one could tell them how to defend better, shoot more accurately, or rebound better. They were uncoachable. They wouldn't listen. So all their God-given talent and ability counted for nothing.

Every instructor knows the dilemma of having a student who won't yield. Every parent knows the pain of having a prodigal who must have his or her way. Where we see failure, wasted opportunities, and heartache, this fatal flaw is invariably present.

The King Who Started Well

It's not always easy to listen. King Amaziah is one of God's poster people for this kind of problem. He is the man who wouldn't listen. The strange thing is that Amaziah *did* listen at first. He listened very closely and obediently to the Word of the Lord when he began his reign as king of Judah.

> Amaziah was twenty-five years old when he became king, and he reigned in Jerusalem twenty-nine years... He did what was right in the eyes of the Lord, but not wholeheartedly. After the kingdom was firmly in his control, he executed the officials who had murdered his father the king. Yet he did not put their sons to death, but acted in accordance with what is written in the Law, in the Book of Moses, where the Lord commanded: "Fathers shall not be put to death for their children, nor children put to death for their fathers; each is to die for his own sins" (2 Chronicles 25:1–4).

After he was established on the throne, Amaziah had to take care of some unfinished business. His father, the late King Joash, had been assassinated, and it was Amaziah's duty to punish the men responsible for this vicious crime. Although he now had absolute power, Amaziah did not give in to the desire for unbridled vengeance by executing the assassins and their families. (This was a common practice during those rough-and-tumble days when royal power wreaked havoc among the peoples of the world.) Rather, King Amaziah heeded the commandment of God found in Deuteronomy 24:16. This commandment limited punishment, no matter how grievous the crime, to only the guilty parties, not their innocent children. So Amaziah listened well to the Word of the Lord.

Another challenge also lay before the king. After organizing and enlarging his army for a major campaign against the Edomites, Amaziah "hired a hundred thousand fighting men from Israel" (2 *Chronicles 25:6*) at the cost of almost four tons of silver! He believed that the three hundred thousand troops from Judah could only be strengthened by adding one hundred thousand mercenaries from the northern kingdom of Israel. Everyone knows that in war, more is better, right? Well, Amaziah found out that God's math was different from his.

A man of God came to him and boldly declared, "These troops from Israel must not march with you, for the Lord is not with Israel" (*v.7*). The northern ten tribes of Israel had given themselves over to gross idolatry, and the anger of Jehovah hung over them. Because of this, Amaziah was forbidden to deploy their forces. If he used them, he was told, "God will overthrow you before the enemy." As the prophet revealed, "God has the power to help or to overthrow" (*v.8*). In other words, more is less if God doesn't bless!

Amaziah was still troubled, though, by the almost four tons of silver that would be wasted if he dismissed the Israelite troops. "But what about the hundred talents I paid for these Israelite troops?" he asked. The prophet replied, "The Lord can give you much more than that" (*v.9*). So the king obediently dismissed the mercenaries. He then led his smaller army—one that had God's blessing—to the Valley of Salt and routed the Edomites.

What joy there was among the troops of Judah that night as they celebrated their impressive victory! What wonderful lessons Amaziah

teaches us as we watch him obeying not only the express commands
of the Law of God but also the prophetic voice of the Spirit of God.
The king's obedience to God's leading in a specific situation, even at
great monetary loss, is a powerful example for us to follow. As the
king listened and obeyed, God was faithful to fulfill his promise of
victory and blessing.

It's Unbelievable—or Is It?

But a very odd thing happened to King Amaziah as he concluded
his campaign against the Edomites. His attention was drawn to the
idols that his defeated foes worshiped. What he did seems too unbe-
lievable to be true: "When Amaziah returned from slaughtering the
Edomites, he brought back the gods of the people of Seir. He set
them up as his own gods, bowed down to them and burned sacrifices
to them. The anger of the Lord burned against Amaziah" (2 *Chronicles
25:14–15*).

How could this happen to a man who was so blessed by God?
The Law of God clearly forbids bowing down to any heathen idol.
The Lord had repeatedly commanded his people to have no other
gods before him (*Exodus 20:3; Deuteronomy 5:7*). These were the ABCs of
religious instruction among the Israelites! But somehow Amaziah's sick
fascination with Edomite idols closed his ears to the Word of the Lord.
Maybe it was his successful reign thus far. Maybe it was his great
victory over the Edomites. We don't know why, but for some reason
the king of Judah stopped measuring his actions against the precepts
of God's Word.

> *Things went from bad to worse, which is what
> usually happens when people turn their backs on God.*

Things went from bad to worse, which is what usually happens
when men and women turn their backs on God. While Amaziah
burned sacrifices to these abominable idols, God's anger burned

against the king's audacious sin. A prophet of the Lord immediately confronted Amaziah with a logical question straight from the throne of God: "Why do you consult this people's gods, which could not save their own people from your hand?" (2 Chronicles 25:15). In other words, God said, "Wake up, Amaziah! These are not only dumb idols, they are the 'loser gods' that did nothing for the Edomites whom I helped you defeat so decisively!" It is incredible how sinful disobedience blinds us to truth, even when it is staring us right in the face.

Amaziah then escalated his stubbornness by rejecting a prophetic message that was sent to save him from his own devices. While the prophet was still speaking, the king said to him, "Have we appointed you an adviser to the king? Stop! Why be struck down?" (v.16). The man who once listened, childlike, to God's voice now arrogantly cut off the prophet's message and threatened to kill him if he went any further. Before he left, the unnamed prophet said something that I pray the Holy Spirit will help us all to remember: "I know that God has determined to destroy you, because you have done this and *have not listened* to my counsel" (v.16).

That was the solemn verdict. Once Amaziah closed his ears to the voice of God, nothing in heaven or on earth could help him. He was doomed because he wouldn't listen.

Amaziah soon unwisely attacked the northern kingdom of Israel. But God's blessing was no longer on him, so his army was routed. Amaziah's victorious enemies broke down about six hundred feet of Jerusalem's walls, seized the gold and silver and sacred articles in the temple, and raided the palace treasury. Hostages were taken from among the people. In the end, the nation of Judah was bankrupt, the temple had been violated, and countless families mourned the loss of husbands and fathers they would never see again. This was the sad legacy of the king who wouldn't listen.

A Great Tragedy

The truth is, no matter how deep our sin is, no matter how far we have fallen, there is still hope if we will just listen to what God is saying. It is when we get so full of ourselves and too busy to stop and listen that we cut ourselves off from the one true Friend who can help us. Our shallowness and self-centeredness make us deaf to words that would bring healing and spiritual life. Even when God sends family members and friends to warn or correct us, our pride often makes us incapable of receiving help. "I thought you were my friend—how could you say that?" is our immature reaction that shows we have completely missed what God was trying to do.

While I was preparing this message on King Amaziah for a Sunday sermon, I spent days meditating and praying about the best way to preach it. Among other things, I asked the Lord to give me a powerful illustration about the horrible sin of not listening to him. I can't say I was ready for or happy with the answer he provided.

Barbara was just a child when I first met her. She was the daughter of a precious couple God sent to our church during the early days of our ministry. Her father was a former alcoholic whom Christ powerfully transformed into a faithful, praying servant of God. Carol and I shared many meals at his home. While we enjoyed rice and beans and other Puerto Rican dishes, Barbara played in the next room with our daughter, Chrissy, who was about the same age.

Years went by, and Barbara's parents decided to move first to Pennsylvania and later retired to Puerto Rico. But problems with Barbara disturbed their otherwise tranquil life.

Barbara showed a nasty streak of rebellion as a teenager, and it got worse as time went on. She became so full of herself, her opinions, and the determination to do her own thing that she barely resembled the sweet girl we had watched grow up. She wouldn't listen to anyone who offered counsel or correction. She told off her family, her youth leaders, and anyone else who seemed to get in her way. I remember one brief encounter I had with her. I was shocked at the hardness of her heart. Barbara believed she had *all* the answers, that was for sure.

After her parents relocated to Puerto Rico, Barbara moved in with a guy and had a couple of kids by him. Their relationship ended, and Barbara moved to another borough of New York City. She was thirty-one and had dropped off the radar screen...until the week I was preparing my sermon on King Amaziah.

In the middle of that week, one of my associate pastors put on my desk two articles from the newspapers. One was from the *New York Post*, another from the *Daily News*. These were not two-line news items but full-blown articles about a horrible crime. And there was Barbara's picture in the middle of the whole mess. She had moved in with a nineteen-year-old guy who obviously had serious problems. The newspaper reported that her three-and-a-half-year-old daughter had been found murdered in the squalid apartment the couple shared. The young man was under arrest without bail, and Barbara was being held in Rikers Island, a very scary prison in which no one would ever want to spend even one night.

So while I was preaching the message "The Man Who Wouldn't Listen" on Sunday, a frightened, heartbroken woman was sobbing in a lonely cell in Rikers Island. But out of this horrible nightmare of sin and spiritual darkness there came a shaft of light. Barbara began to listen, to remember truths about Jesus that were taught to her years ago.

Barbara was released on bail after her arrest and quickly made her way to the Brooklyn Tabernacle. We had the entire congregation pray for her during a Tuesday night prayer meeting as she cried out to God for mercy and pardon. It was a very moving moment as we heard her pray, "Jesus, please forgive me. Help me! Give me another chance."

Barbara later told me that everything started turning sour in her life when she turned away from Jesus. That's when she shut her ears to the truths she had heard growing up and to the loving people who had pleaded with her to turn back to God. Not listening led Barbara into horrible situations she never dreamed of.

In the meantime, the charges against Barbara were bumped up to something far more serious, so she was sent back to prison to await trial. As I write this book, she sits once again in Rikers Island waiting for the outcome of her case. We have many people praying that God will grant mercy toward her, but this one thing we know: Barbara is not alone—and she knows it, too. Once again she is enjoying the peace that comes from listening to the Lord.

Thank God for his amazing loving-kindness.

The Unexpected Letter

Barbara wrote to me from prison as I was still writing this chapter. After reading her letter, I knew it should be included here. She agreed to share it with you, believing that God will use it to wake up someone else to the importance of listening to God. She doesn't want anyone else to experience the heartache and pain she has felt and caused.

Dear Pastor Cymbala,

When you get this letter, I pray that it finds you and your family in good health.

I received the copy of *Fresh Power* that you sent me. I just finished it, and it truly blessed me. Funny, because a few days ago I was praying and asking God how I was supposed to go on without my daughter. But after I read the chapter about the couple in Africa, it was almost as if God was saying, "There's your answer." I doubt if I would be saved today, even though this tragedy was so terrible, without it.

When God took my daughter, he reminded me about how much I loved him at one time, how I trusted and believed in him. I had forgotten, Pastor, all about that. Although my heart hurts because I can't be with her, I know that through her death many people will come to know the Lord. It has already started. I started having Bible studies here in Rikers Island almost every night, and God has brought girls to me left and right.

God has a purpose for me behind these walls, and although I truly hate it here God has made the time go by "better." That's not to say that I don't have my days, because the Lord knows I do. But I know that when I cry out to him he's right there reminding me that he's just a cry away.

Our Bible study has grown. It started with just me and another girl, and now we have about five people coming every night and others who come in just for a little while. You see, I never really understood that verse that says, "You can't serve two masters." Now I do understand it. Before I left the church, I was trying to serve two masters, and I couldn't. The narrow road wasn't as pleasing as that wide one. God is so good, though, because he saved me.

I remember as a little girl I wanted to do nothing but sing, read, and praise him. As I reflect, sitting in my cell, I can see Jesus just sitting there and waiting and waiting and waiting through every heartbreak, through every bad time, while I was getting high to try to forget everything I was going through. He just sat there waiting, almost saying to me, "Call out to me, Barbara. I'll help you. Just call to me." But I didn't. I was too busy....

I don't ever want to have anything to do with anything or anyone that doesn't have to do with God. I worshiped too many other gods, Pastor Cymbala, and they got me to this point.

Anyway, I'm going to stop writing now. I'll call or write later because my pencil is coming to the end of its point. I'll be sending girls from here, Pastor Cymbala, to your church, so please accept them and show them the same love that you have shown me. I tell the girls here that the only way they can change and not go back to their old ways is if they let God be first and trust him for everything. I have told many of them to go and see you guys, and that you all will help them. I hope that's okay. A lot of girls here want to change, but when they get out they go right back to their old lives and surroundings. They really can't change unless God helps them. I hope it's okay that I'm referring them all to you. Please let me know.

Anyway, keep me in your prayers. If it's all right, can you send me something more to read? I would rather read godly things now than the filthy books that they pass around inside the prison here.

I love you. May God bless and keep you.
Barbara.

Cultivate a Listening Heart

The divine message that Isaiah spoke thousands of years ago applies at all times to all people: "*Listen, listen* to me, and eat what is good, and your soul will delight in the richest of fare. *Give ear* and come to me; *hear me*, that your soul may live" *(Isaiah 55:2–3)*. The key to a blessed life is to have a listening heart that longs to know what the Lord is saying.

Think for a moment about the lack of blessing and the increasing hardness of heart in the lives of so many Christians across the country. This emptiness comes primarily from not listening to God. Consider, too, the countless, discouraged pastors who are engrossed in every new fad and formula that comes from men but who spend little time waiting on God, waiting to hear the Holy Spirit's directives for their ministries. God is a speaking, communicating God, but someone has to be listening on the other end.

God is a speaking, communicating God,
but someone has to be listening on the other end.

Jesus wrote letters to seven different churches in the book of Revelation. The spiritual condition of each assembly was different, and therefore Christ's words were never the same as he addressed their unique situations. But it is noteworthy that he used the *same* phrase to close *all* seven letters: "He who has an ear, let him *hear* what the Spirit says to the churches" *(Revelation 2–3)*.

The Holy Spirit still speaks vital messages to God's people today, but we must have tender, attentive hearts to hear what he is saying.

When was the last time you and I could say that we *heard* from God? This is not some far-out, fanatical mysticism; it is a life-and-death issue that will affect our lives here on earth and determine our eternal destiny. God is still pleading in countless ways, "Hear me, that your soul may live" *(Isaiah 55:3)*. Don't all of us need to slow down and get quiet before him? What benefit is there in anything else if we are not hearing what our Creator is saying to us?

God's eyes still roam over the earth looking for attentive, submissive hearts so he can show himself strong and mighty on our behalf. Let's ask God for the blessing of a childlike heart such as young Samuel had, so that when the Lord calls our name we, too, can answer, "Speak, for your servant is listening" *(1 Samuel 3:10)*.

Lord, help us to have a listening heart that is soft and teachable.
Save us from being so filled with ourselves that we can't hear you.
Give us the grace to both listen and obey when you speak to us. Amen.

Severe Gifts

Fire-Testing Seasons from a Loving Father

Gary Thomas

The Church is the one thing that saves a man from the
degrading servitude of being a child of his time.
G.K. Chesterton

"Did you hear about Mike?"

"No," I said. "What happened?"

When I arrived on Western Washington University's campus in 1980, Mike Dittman was perhaps the most dynamic Christian I had ever met. He was several years older than I was, and already a leader in the college ministry I attended. Mike had everything: a charismatic personality, great athletic ability, and a walk of integrity, as well as being a skilled worship leader and a good teacher. He could lead you into the presence of God like few I've ever met. I often sought him out at lunchtime to talk, and was later pleased to end up being in the small group he led.

Following his time at Western, Mike served as a campus pastor and then enrolled in graduate studies to become a counselor. He worked at a church for a number of years until finally an "intervention" of sorts took place. Men whom Mike respected and loved confronted him and said, "Mike, you're very competent. Very insightful. A dynamic leader. A guy who inspires admiration and respect. But you're also too blunt. You hurt people with your words. You lack compassion and empathy."

Mike was devastated, but in a good way. He realized that not one of the positive traits mentioned by these men was a "fruit of the Spirit," and he found himself praying, "God, I wish I was a little less 'dynamic' and a little more compassionate."

It was just a couple years later that a close friend told me the shocking news: After a morning workout, Mike's body dropped to the locker room floor. A brain hemorrhage almost took his life, but after a furious scare, doctors were able to keep Mike in this world—albeit, a very different Mike.

His Hollywood-handsome appearance was gone. Half of Mike's face now looks "fallen," pulled over to one side. He can't sing anymore or play his guitar, so there's no more leading worship. For a while his speech was slurred, so he couldn't teach. He was humbled in just about every way an ambitious man can be humbled.

After months of grueling therapy, Mike moved on. The devastating effect on his body was paralleled by an equally powerful—and wonderful—change in his spirit. Now, years later, Mike's ministry has never been more productive. He started a phenomenally successful department of counseling at the Philadelphia Biblical University, which has grown from a handful of students to hundreds of participants. People fly in to Philadelphia from all over the country to meet with Mike—pastors who have fallen, marriages that have broken apart, children who are rebelling. Mike's seen it all. Whereas before his focus was on the masses, Mike now specializes in healing hurting hearts, one at a time.

"The brain hemorrhage took a lot away from me," Mike told me recently, "but it gave me even more." Mike is now the type of guy whose spirit invites you to quiet your heart, get rid of all pretenses, and revel in God's presence. I think the main difference is that in college, when I was around Mike, I wanted to be like Mike. Now, after spending time with Mike, I want to be more like Jesus.

The amazing thing is that Mike's story, though inspirational, is not particularly unique. I have heard so many Christians tell me of a gut-wrenching season they walked through, only to hear them say, "In the end, I'm glad it happened. The fruit it creates far outweighs the pain and angst that come with it."

> *These seasons are necessary because we do not walk easily into maturity.*

None of them would have chosen ahead of time to walk through such a difficult trial. But all of them are grateful, in hindsight, that the trial came. Such fire-testing seasons are severe gifts from a loving Father, though initially they are rarely received as such.

These seasons are necessary because we do not walk easily into maturity. At first, Christianity can be an intoxicating blend of freedom, joy, exuberance, and newfound discovery. Longtime sins drop off us with relatively little effort. Bible study is rich; we may feel like archaeologists finally coming across an unexplored cave as we become astonished at the insights that pour from the book in front of us. Intimacy, tears, and the assurance of God's voice and guidance mark our times of prayer.

This "spiritual infatuation" phase is well known and well documented among spiritual directors and those familiar with spiritual formation. Just like romantic infatuation is self-centered, so spiritual infatuation tends to be "all about me." It *seems* as though it's all about God, but the focus of new believers' lives is still mostly taken up with how they're doing with regard to defeating sins, as well as cultivating the new joy and spiritual depth that come from walking with God. They're thrilled with what Christianity has done *for them.*

Eventually, God asks us to discard this infatuation and move on to a mature friendship with him. In a true friendship, it's no longer "all about me." It's about partnering with God to build his kingdom. That means, first, being "fire-tested" and, second, growing in ways that we naturally wouldn't be inclined to grow. This growth can be painful for us, but it's a growth that is necessary if we are to become the type of women and men whom God can use. Instead of focusing on our desire for God to answer our prayers, spiritual maturity leads us to

> *The first sign that a believer has failed to move in a timely fashion past the spiritual infatuation stage is usually disillusionment.*

yearn for faithfulness, Christlikeness, and others-centeredness. This is a painful process, a very real spiritual death that some have described as being "born again" *again,* except for the fact that it is never a onetime event.

It is a mistake to ask someone to grow out of spiritual infatuation too quickly. Such a season has its place. There's no getting around the fact that babies need diapers and milk. But when a ten-, twenty-, or thirty-year-old still wears diapers and still acts as though the world revolves around his or her own personal happiness, something has gone wrong.

The first sign that a believer has failed to move in a timely fashion past the spiritual infatuation stage is usually *disillusionment*. Whereas before they thought of God as only kind, only merciful, and only loving, they now tend to view him as stubborn, severe, and unyielding. A wise spiritual director will seek to lay the groundwork for a new way of thinking during this stage. There's a place for this disillusionment, provided it effects the sea change that leads to mature friendship with God. If disillusionment remains, however, it ceases to motivate and eventually may bury the believer under its despair.

The second mark is an ongoing *what's in it for me personally?* attitude. We live in a "me-first" culture, and we often try to individualize corporate promises, largely because we're more concerned about what the Bible says to us individually than about how it calls us to live in community—that is, as those who are a part of the church. Peter tells us that, corporately, we are "a chosen people, a royal priesthood, a holy nation, a people belonging to God." Why? Not for any individual purpose, but for a corporate one that honors God: "that you may declare the praises of him who called you out of darkness into his wonderful light. Once you were not a people, but now you are the people of God; once you had not received mercy, but now you have received mercy" (1 Peter 2:9–10).

> The new groundwork that needs to be laid is an authentic faith that is base on a God-centered life.

When God calls us to himself, he calls us to his church, to a purpose bigger than ourselves. This may sound shocking to some, but biblically, living for God means living for his church. There is a glory in the presence of Jesus Christ, seen when believers come together, that will necessarily be missing in an individual pursuit of God. When the gospel is turned from a community-centered faith to an individual-centered faith ("Jesus would have died for me if I had been the only one!"), we eclipse much of its power and meaning.

The new groundwork that needs to be laid is an authentic faith that is based on a God-centered life. Rather than the believer being the sun around whom God, the church, and the world revolve in order to create a happy, easy, and prosperous life, God becomes the sun around which the believer revolves, a believer who is willing to suffer—even to be persecuted—and lay down his or her life to build God's kingdom and to serve God's church. This is a radical shift—indeed, the most radical (and freeing) shift known in human experience—and it leads to a deep friendship with God.

Friendship with God

In relationships, even our best intentions can go ridiculously awry. I read of one man who thought he had planned the perfect date with his wife: "For Valentine's Day," he wrote, "I decided to take my wife out for a nice romantic dinner, and all she did was complain. Next time I want to eat at Hooters, I'll go by myself." We can bring this same self-centeredness into our relationship with God. Much of what we say, or even think, we're doing on God's behalf is really being done for ourselves.

On a deeper level, I believe many of us are hungry and thirsty for a faith based on sacrifice instead of on self-absorption and simplistic denial. We don't want to become Christians in order to become an *improved* man or woman, but an *entirely new* man or woman—people who live with a different outlook on life, who find joy while others pursue happiness, who find meaning in what others see as something to simply be overcome or cured, who want to drink deeply of life— with its mountains and valleys, twists and turns—rather than to "rise above it."

This is an authentic faith, prescribed for a disillusioned world. It is a faith taught by Jesus, passed on by the ancients, and practiced throughout two thousand years of church history. It's our heritage, our birthright, and our blessing. It has been witnessed to as ultimately the most fulfilling life ever lived, though it is frequently a life of hardship and difficulty.

To embrace God's love and kingdom is to embrace his broken, passionate heart. It is to expose ourselves to the assaults brought on by the world's hatred toward God. The active Christian life is a life full of risks, heartaches, and responsibilities. God does indeed bear our burdens. Certainly, he blesses us in many ways, but this initial relief is for the purpose of assigning to us more

> *To embrace God's love and kingdom is to embrace his broken, passionate heart*

important concerns than our own. Only this time, we weep not because our house is too small or because we have overextended our credit, but because we are taxed to the limit as we reach out to a hurting world. Yes, we experience peace, joy, and hope, but it is a peace in the midst of turmoil, a joy marked with empathy, and a hope refined by suffering.

Ultimately, spiritual maturity is not about memorizing the Bible and mastering the spiritual disciplines. These are healthy things to do, but they are still only means to a greater end, which in itself is *learning to love with God's love* and *learning to serve with God's power*. In a fallen world, love begs to be unleashed—a love that is supernatural in origin, without limit, a love that perseveres in the face of the deepest hatred or the sharpest pain. It is a love that becomes silhouetted in a broken world, framed by human suffering, illuminated in an explosion of God's presence breaking into a dark cellar.

In a world where suffering and difficulty are certain, friendship with God frees us from being limited by what we don't have, by what we are suffering, or by what we are enduring. Mature friendship with God reminds us that our existence is much broader than our suffering and difficulty. God doesn't offer us freedom *from* a broken world; instead, he offers us

> *Friendship with God frees us from being limited by what we don't have, by what we are suffering, or by what we are enduring.*

friendship with himself as we walk *through* a fallen world—and those who persevere will find that this friendship is worth more, so very much more, than anything this fallen world can offer.

In short, we are missing out when we insist on self-absorption, affluence, and ease over against pursuing a deeper walk with God. We miss out on an intimacy that has been heralded by previous generations, a fellowship of labor, suffering, persecution, and selflessness. It doesn't sound like much fun initially, but those who have walked these roads have left behind a witness that they have reached an invigorating, soul-satisfying land. These women and men testify to being radically satisfied in God, even though others may scratch their heads as they try to figure out how someone who walks such a difficult road could possibly be happy.

In a broken, fallen world, we really only have two choices: mature friendship with God, or radical disillusionment.

A Classical Faith

Today's self-oriented gospel is no stranger to the church. In fact, it is relatively similar to the faith that spawned the Christian flight to the desert in the fourth century, the spread of monasticism in the sixth century, the reform of monasticism in the Middle Ages, and then the spread of Puritanism in the seventeenth century. Throughout history, God has always left his witness of a "classical faith"—that is, a God-centered, authentic faith. Not the faith of the Pharisees, who majored on the minors and made legalistic obedience their god; not the faith of those who see God as their ticket to comfort and ease; nor yet the faith that sees Christianity as still another means to "improve ourselves" and become "more disciplined." God has served us and does serve us—but ultimately, classical, authentic Christianity is about glorifying, proclaiming, adoring, and obeying God.

> In a broken, fallen world, we really only have two choices: mature friendship with God, or radical disilusionment.

If you've found yourself disillusioned in any way with Christianity or with your faith in God, make sure it's really Christianity you're disillusioned with and not some perversion of it that is only masquerading as faith. Check to see if you are caught in the crossroads of moving beyond spiritual infatuation, and being invited into the quieter—and, quite frankly, seemingly darker—waters of mature friendship with God. Authentic Christianity majors on a powerful display of God's presence, often through his people, in a world that is radically broken.

Authentic faith penetrates the most unlikely of places. This faith is found, for instance, when we die to ourselves and put others first. Such a faith is nurtured when we cultivate contentment instead of spending our best energy and efforts to improve our lot in life. Classical faith is strengthened in suffering, persecution, waiting, and even mourning. Just as surely as water seeks the lowest point in the land, so such a faith seeks the least of all people. Instead of holding on to grudges, authentic faith chooses forgiveness. Authentic faith lives with another world in mind, recognizing that what we do in this broken world will be judged.

The "authentic disciplines," as I call them, differ from the traditional spiritual disciplines in that the authentic disciplines are, for the most part, initiated outside of us.[1] God brings them into our life when he wills and as he wills. Just by reading about suffering doesn't bring you through suffering—you can't *make* these disciplines happen, as you can make fasting or meditation take place. This is a God-ordained spirituality, dependent on his sovereignty.

The traditional disciplines—fasting, meditation, study, prayer, and the like—are all crucial elements of building our faith, but let's be honest. They can also foster pride, arrogance, self-sufficiency, religiosity, and worse. Their benefit is clearly worth the risk, but that's why the authentic disciplines are such a helpful and even vital addition; they turn us away from human effort—from men and women seeking the face of God—and turn us back toward God seeking the face of men and women.

There's no pride left when God takes me through a time of suffering. There's no self-righteousness when I am called to wait. There is no religiosity when I am truly mourning. This is a spirituality I can't control, I can't initiate, I can't bring about. It is a radical dependence on God's husbandry. All I can do is try to appreciate it and learn from it. The rest—the duration of the trial, the intensity of the trial, the ultimate cessation of the trial—is almost always up to him.

When we live with such an authentic faith, in a mature friendship with God, we cultivate what I like to call a "defiant beauty."

Defiant Beauty

I once spoke at a married couple's retreat in southwestern Washington. To get there I had to travel through "tree country," miles and miles of tree farms planted by Weyerhaeuser, one of North America's largest producers of timber. Each farm had a sign announcing, "These trees were planted in 1988." "These trees were planted in 1992." "These trees were planted in 1996."

Interspersed among the tree farms were occasional stretches of clear-cut logging projects. I love trees, and perhaps because of that, I find few things more ugly than a clear-cut stretch of land. It looks devastated, broken, and abused. I know that, after planting, the land will come back, but it's still sad to see such brutal scarring of a forest.

As I drove up the highway, I passed yet another clear-cut stretch when my eye suddenly caught something that almost made me pull off the road. There, in a devastated patch of land, stood a startlingly beautiful maple tree in full autumn colors. Somehow, the loggers had missed it.

The contrast could not have been more stark and, for that reason, more beautiful. Beauty surrounded by beauty begins, after a time, to seem mediocre. Beauty in the midst of chaos or ugliness is stunning. It's onstage, and it seizes your attention. In a barren, broken stretch of land, this tree captured my imagination and told another story. Had it been in the midst of New Hampshire's White Mountains during autumn, it likely would have been missed—one stunning tree in a forest of stunning trees blends right in. Here, in a broken, hurting land, this glorious tree proclaimed a transcendent truth.

In the deepest part of us, we truly yearn, I believe, for such "defiant beauty." In a world where people live self-centered lives, where ugly things happen, where sin seems to spread unchecked, where daily assaults take their toll, we can point to the defiant beauty of a selfless life, seeking first the kingdom of God, putting others first, and even sacrificing ourselves in the process, if need be—all to proclaim a transcendent truth that is greater than ourselves.

> *In a world where people live self-centered lives, we can point to the defiant beauty of a selfless life.*

In this book, I'm going to invite you to develop a defiant beauty—the kind of defiant beauty that has shone through all generations of the church. At some points in our history, the beauty has been marred and partially hidden. But it's always been there. It's our legacy, and this is an invitation to pick it back up once again.

Authentic Faith

Following Lee's surrender to Grant at Appomattox during the waning days of the Civil War, the son of Henry Wise, an ex-Southern governor, told his father that he had taken the loyalty oath to the United States.

"You have disgraced the family, sir!" Henry Wise responded.

The son, a former captain in the Confederate Army, was mortified and pled his case: "But, Father, General Lee advised me to do it."

Hardly a moment passed before Wise recanted. "That alters the case," he told his son. "Whatever General Lee advises is right."

There may be some assertions in this book that, at first glance, don't seem right; they may lead you to ask, "Does Christianity really involve that?" My appeal to you is the same one made by Henry Wise's son: I ask you to consider who first said these words. I have purposely filled this book with more Scripture than any of my previous books, and I have worked just as diligently to root these thoughts and concepts in the precedence of the Christian classics, showing how each tenet was supported, affirmed, and taught by classical Christian writers throughout the centuries. [2]

Mine is not the role of a *pioneer,* much as this title sounds exalted for an author. To my chagrin, a far more honest description for what I'm doing is that of a *tour guide,* taking us through long-ago discovered truths and helping visitors discover their meaning for today. If at first these ideas seem to go against common sense, if some seem to be outdated or impossible to believe, my answer is to point back to these authorities.

What I hope you will find is an authentic faith that rings true throughout the ages. Some of the truths may sound hard, but they are the prescription we need in order to live a truly meaningful and productive life in Christ. And they are a sure remedy for the disillusionment that eventually arises whenever we discard God's truth for an immature, self-centered faith. Even more important, though, together they construct a time-tested pathway to a deeper and more mature friendship with God.

1. This is not true of forgiveness, of course, but even here; forgiveness requires a prior act that someone else has done before we have anything to forgive. Even social mercy requires the presence of someone else who needs our help.

2. Because all of my books incorporate the Christian classics, I'm often asked to define just what a Christian classic is. In a time when the average shelf life of any book is somewhere between milk and yogurt, a Christian classic is a book that has been recognized as helpful and is still being read decades or even centuries after its first publication. There is no "definitive" canon (though I list several classics on my Web site, www.garythomas.com), but there is a generally accepted grouping that includes writers such as Augustine, John Climacus, Teresa of Avila, John of the Cross, Jeanne Guyon, Francis de Sales, John Calvin, William Law, and many, many others.

LIVING BEYOND YOUR SELF

The Discipline of Selflessness

Gary Thomas

Assurance is not to be obtained as much
by self-examination as it is by action.
JONATHAN EDWARDS

In late August 1992, Hurricane Andrew ripped through southern Florida, leveling many homes and buildings that had stood in its path. In the quiet aftermath, a young mother stepped out onto her porch to survey the damage with her little six-year-old boy named Timmy. The young woman looked at the community that used to be, amazed at the rubble that had replaced so many homes, and then she began to wonder, *What could be going through the mind of this young child, seeing such severe destruction?*

Timmy saw his mother looking down at him, and he got nervous, so before she could ask him, he piped up and said, "I didn't do it!"

It's human nature for a young child to survey devastating destruction and have his first thought be, "Don't blame me!" We grow up thinking of ourselves first: How does this affect *me*? What will this mean for *my* life? When we're at our selfish worst, world hunger could be solved, world peace could be ushered in, and cancer could be cured—all within the space of twenty-four hours—but if our hair doesn't do exactly what we want it to, it's an awful, horrible day.

> *There's a clarity to our vision when we completely forget ourselves and concentrate solely on the task before us.*

If we fail to grow out of this self-obsession, it can become a character cancer, quieter and far more subtle than Hurricane Andrew, but ultimately no less destructive spiritually.

On the flip side, there's a clarity to our vision when we completely forget ourselves and concentrate solely on the task before us. It's an energizing feeling to be so focused on someone else that there is no thought of our own welfare or problems. Though it seems ironic, it's a blessed state, far more meaningful than when we are obsessed with our own trials and tribulations—but it's not one that naturally colors our spirit. In fact, I can think of many times when selfishness reigned in my heart.

"Hurry up!" I called out to my family once. "Get into the car! If we don't get moving, there won't be any good seats left!"

Our church has a problem that is simultaneously wonderful and frustrating: The services are packed, and if you don't get there early, you may have to sit in the overflow area. It was an Easter Sunday, and I had expected the services to be even more crowded than usual. My number one goal that morning was to get us to church in time to get decent seats.

I gathered my car keys, only semi-patiently waiting for my wife to finish drying her hair and my daughter to find her shoes. "I put them right by the door," Kelsey insisted. "Somebody must have *stolen* them!"

"Right, Kelsey," I answered. "Someone broke in last night, forgot about the TV, the VCR, and the computer, ignored my wallet sitting in the kitchen, and grabbed a used pair of little girl's size 7 shoes."

"Well, it's *possible!*" she hollered.

> Our fallen nature and the values of our culture collide with the force of an avalanche to push us ever further down the hill of self-centerness.

Walking out to the car, I had just a moment's pause when God's voice broke into my hurried, frenzied spirit. I realized that many of the people I wanted to "beat out" for a good seat would probably be visitors. Our church uses Easter to its fullest evangelistic effect, and God gently spoke to me about my selfish desire to enjoy good worship at the expense of a nonbeliever having the best chance to respond to the gospel. There's nothing wrong with trying to get to church on time, but my competitive nature spit into the face of what our church was trying to do that very morning.

Self-centeredness can creep up on us in so many ways—including wanting to get good seats in church! Our fallen nature and the values of our culture collide with the force of an avalanche to push us ever further down the hill of self-centeredness, but authentic faith calls us back to the summit—and joy—of selflessness.

The Most Meaningful Life Imaginable

Many years ago, *The New Yorker* ran a cartoon in which a smiling woman was jabbering nonstop to a glum-faced companion. The smiling woman finally says, "Well, that's enough about me. Now let's talk about you. What do *you* think about *me*?"

The apostle Paul had an entirely different perspective. Instead of being preoccupied by what others thought of him, Paul learned the theme song of an authentic faith that is to be oriented around the needs of others: "We who are strong ought to bear with the failings of the weak and not to please ourselves. Each of us should please his neighbor for his good, to build him up. For even Christ did not please himself..." *(Romans 15:1–3)*.

In fact, Paul took this line of thinking to a radical and somewhat shocking conclusion: "Though I am free and belong to no man, *I make myself a slave to everyone*, to win as many as possible" *(1 Corinthians 9:19, emphasis added)*. This is an astonishing statement when you consider the context behind it. Paul was a "king" in his culture. Though he faced enemies, to be sure, Paul was often treated with respect and adulation. In Lystra, he was even worshiped as a god *(see Acts 14:8–13)*. Furthermore, as a Pharisee Paul had daily prayed the traditional prayer that went something like this: "Dear God, thank you for not making me a Gentile, a slave, or a woman." Before he met Christ, Paul spent every day of his life thanking God that he wasn't a slave, and now he happily proclaims to the Corinthians that God has turned him into one!

This is the defining difference in Paul's life. He didn't improve on his morality after meeting Christ, because Pharisees went out of their way to live blameless lives. Paul didn't pray more as a Christian, because Pharisees were devoted to regular and public prayer. Paul didn't fast more, because Pharisees were masters of spiritual discipline. The only real difference in Paul's life is that he became centered on the freedom of Christ's provision, which enabled him to love God by serving others instead of being obsessed about his own religious achievements.

> *The only real difference in Paul's life is that he became centered on the freedom of Christ's provision.*

The extreme way in which Paul adhered to this selflessness is, in fact, shocking to modern sensibilities. He tells the Romans that he wishes he could cut himself off from salvation, if by doing so he might save Israel (*see Romans 9:3*). Let's not quickly pass over this. Paul was fully aware of hell's horrors—the physical pain, the emotional angst, the spiritual alienation, separation from loving relationships for all eternity—yet he proclaimed, "I wish I could be damned in hell for all eternity, if, in the twilight before I enter hell, I can look over my shoulder and see the nation of Israel marching into heaven."

Moses prays roughly the same prayer in Exodus 32:32: "But now, please forgive their sin—but if not, then blot me out of the book you have written." Both leaders had such tremendous concern for the people under their charge that they would have placed their own salvation beneath the people's welfare. The examples of Moses, Jesus (whose death was actually redemptive), and Paul safely make this a distinguishing mark of authentic faith.

Could you pray that prayer? I'm not sure I could. Could you willingly agree to spend eternity apart from loved ones and instead enter into an eternity surrounded by hatred, spite, jealousy, bitterness, and lust, separated from your children, grandchildren, parents, and close friends and existing entirely apart from the comfort, mercy, and grace of God? The very thought chills me to my core, yet such was Paul's love for others that he says he would gladly have made that trade.

Where did Paul get this selflessness? How could a man become so humble, so others-oriented, so willing to play the role of a servant? I believe it essentially comes down to this: Paul took the words of Jesus "It is more blessed to give than to receive" (*Acts 20:35*) literally, and he found that they were true! Throughout his letters, Paul is effusive with his thanks and affection for others. Clearly, his service on their behalf brings tremendous joy to his life: "I thank my God through Jesus Christ for all of you" (*Romans 1:8; see 1 Corinthians 1:4*). "For I wrote you out of great distress and anguish of heart and with many tears, not to grieve you but to let you know the depth of my love for you" (*2 Corinthians 2:4*). "It is right for me to feel this way about all of you, since I have you in my heart" (*Philippians 1:7*).

I confess to being somewhat in awe of Paul, particularly when I pause to think about how many communities Paul stayed in touch with and how many different churches he was genuinely concerned about. Paul's letters reveal an ongoing, passionate, and truly concerned relationship with churches spanning the Mediterranean Sea—from Rome to Corinth, Galatia, Ephesus, Philippi, Colosse, and Thessalonica (this in addition to maintaining fervid relationships with individuals such as Timothy, Titus, and dozens of women and men mentioned at the end of his letters—not to mention a lowly slave named Onesimus, on whose behalf Paul took time, while in prison, to write a letter). It is truly amazing to see not just the depth, but the breadth of Paul's active love shown to so many different churches and individuals. One gets the impression that he couldn't have had much else going on in his life, for if he had, he wouldn't have had the emotional energy left to be actively compassionate, loving, and involved with so many people.

> *Paul took the words of Jesus "It is more blessed to give than to receive" literally, and he found that they were true.*

Yet nowhere does this affection seem obligatory. Paul's concern for others was real; the enjoyment he derived from serving them and sacrificing for them was tangible and at times intense. These are not the words of a man who only serves grudgingly. These are the words of a man who has found service to be the most meaningful life imaginable.

So we ask ourselves: Do we, as Peter urges us, truly "love the brotherhood of believers" (1 Peter 2:17)? I'm not talking about "love" in the all too American sense, offering a casual "how are you doing?" while not really caring about the answer. How concerned are we, truly, about God's church, and what sacrifices are we making on its behalf to give evidence to that love? Are we so busy with personal, individual pursuits that our passion for the church has dimmed?

The Christlike life is not simply about practicing impeccable morality and overcoming temptation and faithfully performing a few spiritual disciplines. All of these were done by the Pharisees far more faithfully than any of us will ever perform them, and yet Christ himself said these religious zealots had missed God's intention. To experience

Christ's joy, passion, and fulfillment, we need to adopt an entirely new *mind-set* and *motivation*: We are invited to join our Lord in living for the glory of the Father instead of for our own reputation, and we are called to give ourselves over to the salvation and sanctification of Christ's bride, the church, rather than to be consumed by our own welfare. This holy self-forgetfulness is the most genuine mark of true faith, the evidence of God's merciful grace in our lives.[1]

Paul defiantly took his passion for God several steps further than modern society believes is healthy. He didn't just love Christ, he was nearly consumed by his commitment to his Savior and to the church. His goal and motivation are clearly laid out for us: "And [Christ] died for all, that those who live *should no longer live for themselves* but for him who died for them and was raised again" (*2 Corinthians 5:15, emphasis added*).

Everything Paul experienced was put through this grid. He even learned to rejoice in suffering, because by suffering "I fill up in my flesh what is still lacking in regard to Christ's afflictions, for the sake of his body, which is the church" (*Colossians 1:24*).

Paul didn't look at what hardship did to *him*; he was entirely preoccupied by what his suffering accomplished for *God's church*. When he was imprisoned, Paul took heart in the fact that "because of my chains, most of the brothers in the Lord have been encouraged to speak the word of God more courageously and fearlessly" (*Philippians 1:14*).

> *The key to experiencing Paul's joy is adopting Paul's mission, which is to become a champion of God's work on this earth. Selflessness seasons our faith with meaning and applies purpose to our pain.*

The key to experiencing Paul's joy is adopting Paul's mission, which is to become a champion of God's work on this earth. Ironically, this attitude of selflessness actually creates a fountain of joy: "A generous man will prosper; he who refreshes others will himself be refreshed" (*Proverbs 11:25*). Selflessness seasons our faith with meaning and applies purpose to our pain. If we sacrifice, serve, and tirelessly work to build the kingdom of God in this world, we will find, as did Paul and the ancients, that the selfless life, though not an easy life, though filled with much pain, anguish, and heartache, is the most meaningful life that can be lived.

When you know you're doing something solely out of love for God and a desire to see his kingdom prosper on this earth, there's an unrivaled inner satisfaction that fills your soul. This satisfaction has been testified to for ages, beginning with the classical Christian writers.

The Classical Chorus

Augustine captured the spirit of Paul when he wrote that "God fashions us, that is, forms and creates us anew, not as men—for he has done that already—but as good men, which His grace is now doing, that we may be a new creation in Christ Jesus."[2] In other words, when God's Spirit transforms us and re-creates us, he does so with a view toward making us less selfish and more inclined to serve others—that is, to make us good. He doesn't just save us, but intends to change us. What else is the meaning of Paul's words, "For we are God's workmanship, created in Christ Jesus *to do good works*, which God prepared in advance for us to do" *(Ephesians 2:10, emphasis added)*.

But here's the delightful irony: In Augustine's mind, acts of goodwill and charity, far from being a nuisance and a burden, actually promote true happiness: "Acts of compassion...towards our neighbors, when they are directed towards God...are intended to free us from misery and thus to bring us to happiness—which is only attained by that good of which it has been said, 'As for me, my true good is to cling to God' *(Psalm 73:28)*."[3]

Augustine had plenty of opportunities to apply this line of thinking. When he first became a Christian, Augustine's ambition was to become a quiet monk, living out his final days in prayer and contemplation. He had had enough of fast living, and he was ready to live the meditative life. His piety became noticed in high places, however, and church authorities soon asked Augustine to become a bishop, which led him into a very public life—the opposite of what he wanted. How many of us have felt this same tug. Perhaps you're a private person, called into a form of service and ministry you know God is leading you into, but it's something you would never choose on your own. That's the situation Augustine was in, and he responded in obedience.

Although this selflessness led Augustine into a life of great joy, meaning, and purpose, it also ultimately led him to his death. In 427, the Arian Vandals advanced into North Africa, where Augustine lived and ministered. Genserik, the Vandal king, specifically sought out Christian churches, as he had heard they were particularly rich with treasures. Refugees poured into Hippo, where Augustine was serving, and it wasn't long before Genserik had laid siege to Augustine's city.

The refugees not only brought heightened responsibilities for Augustine, they also brought disease. In the fifth century, so many people packed into so tight a space inevitably created a sick environment. At this point, Augustine had three choices: He could flee (as bishop, Augustine could have abandoned his people and his post and sought safe sanctuary elsewhere in the kingdom), he could stay holed

> *The ancients were not masochists; they wanted true joy like all of us do.*

up in his palace and ignore the needs of his people but perhaps preserve his own health, or he could go out, get his hands dirty, and risk becoming ill himself.

Augustine didn't know how to be a bishop from afar, so he kept up his active schedule, being present with the people—and paid dearly for his service. During the third month of the siege, in August of 430, Augustine developed a high fever from which he never recovered. This powerful man of God, whose books Christians still read because of their logic, power, passion, and faith, gave his last hours ministering to the most basic needs of a frightened flock.

God didn't re-create us to be men and women—he's done that already—but to become *good* men and women.

The literature of the classics is a veritable chorus of dying to self so that we might truly live. The ancients were not masochists; they wanted true joy like all of us do. Certainly, they sought fulfillment, and even happiness, but they discovered that happiness is best experienced in a selfless life, that self-centered living creates its own misery —and they were quite literally willing to bet their lives on it.

In *Beyond Personality*, C. S. Lewis writes the following:

> The principle runs through all life from top to bottom. Give up yourself, and you'll find your real self. Lose your life and you'll save it. Submit to death, death of your ambitions and favorite wishes every day and death of your whole body in the end: submit with every fiber of your being, and you will find eternal life. Keep

nothing back. Nothing that you have not given away will ever be really yours. Nothing in you that has not died will ever be raised from the dead. Look for yourself, and you will find in the long run only hatred, loneliness, despair, rage, ruin, and decay. But look for Christ and you will find Him, and with Him everything else thrown in.[4]

This is why the self-centered "gospel" is so disillusioning. In the long run, living only for comfort, pleasure, and ease—even using religion to do so—leads only to "hatred, loneliness, despair, rage, ruin, and decay." Dying to ourselves and living solely for God and his kingdom, being enlisted to do good to others and focus on serving, gives us God, and in God we have everything.

Like Augustine, Lewis knew what he was talking about when he spoke of the benefit that comes from selfless living. During the Second World War, Lewis took in numerous children who were fleeing London and other cities vulnerable to German bombing. Bringing children into the Kilns was a lot of extra work—not to mention coping with the excess noise. Be careful not to look at Lewis's sacrifice too lightly. As a writer, I work out of my home, so I can imagine what it would be like to try to prepare college courses and keep writing books and articles and respond to correspondence while there are unruly kids running around the house (kids who miss their parents). Certainly, Lewis must have realized that his work would take a severe beating. Yet, in actuality, this act of sacrifice helped produce Lewis's most famous writings.

You see, one afternoon one of these evacuated children grew interested in an old wardrobe and asked Lewis if, perhaps, there was anything behind it. Thus was planted the seed for perhaps the most beloved of all of

> *Dying to ourselves and living solely for God and his kingdom gives us God, and in God we have everything.*

Lewis's books, *The Lion, the Witch, and the Wardrobe*. George Sayer, one of Lewis's biographers, writes of this period, "Having children in the house benefited [Lewis] immensely. He had been shy and ignorant of them, but he now gradually acquired the knowledge and affection for them that made it possible for him to write the Narnia books.

Without their presence, it is unlikely that he would even have had the impulse."[5]

If you think selfless living is costly, you haven't honestly considered the even higher price we pay for living a selfish life. We may never know how many powerful times of ministry we've missed out on as we focused only on ourselves.

The Truly "Happy" State

Being a professional athlete makes you an object of love or hate. Rarely are you allowed to swim in the middle. When you're playing well, the fans love you. When you're having a bad season, the fans think you're an overpaid bum.

The precariousness of such a livelihood tempts many athletes to become extremely self-centered, but major league pitcher Orel Hershiser found a better way. In the late eighties and early nineties, Orel was about as accomplished as a pitcher can get. During one stretch, he pitched a major-league-record 59 consecutive scoreless innings—that's almost 7 straight games—an astonishing run by any measure. In 1988, he won the National League Cy Young Award (given annually to the league's outstanding pitcher) and was voted the World Series Most Valuable Player.

In short, Hershiser had a lot of "stock." Young players looked up to him as the model of what they wanted to achieve. Players can use this cache to either lord it over others or to serve, and Orel took the latter approach.

After the Los Angeles Dodgers spring training camp ended in 1992, a young, skinny pitcher felt devastated after being demoted to the minor leagues. When the young pitcher's head was turned, Orel quietly slipped a ball into his bag. On the ball, Orel had written, "From one big leaguer to another. See you back here soon."

> "From one big leaguer to another. See you back here soon."

Imagine being that discouraged pitcher, wondering if you'll ever get another chance, and then reaching into your bag when you get home and having the most accomplished pitcher of your day write, "From one big leaguer to another." Even more encouraging, Orel showed his confidence in the young man's potential when he added, "See you back here soon."

Orel's words proved prophetic. That skinny pitcher's name was Pedro Martinez, now considered by many to be the best pitcher in all of baseball. At the time of this writing, he had the lowest earned run average in the entire major leagues.

Hershiser retired during the 2000 baseball season, but now that his own pitching career is over, he can take joy from the fact that he helped encourage a fellow player to not give up. In a sense, his influence lives on through a fiery pitcher who can often seem unbeatable.

When our happiness is dependent on what happens to us and when our self-focus determines our daily mood, our joy will necessarily be limited to whatever good thing happens to us. But when we learn to truly delight in the welfare of others and rejoice in what God is doing in their lives, the potential for increased joy skyrockets. Even when Paul was in prison, he could rejoice over what God was doing in Colosse. As death drew near, Paul took joy in the rise of Timothy's ministry. And as persecution followed upon persecution, Paul rejoiced at the strength and witness of the Philippians. Because Paul was so others-focused, nothing could get him down. There was always someone to rejoice about and to thank God for! This is the incredible miracle of joy that springs forth when an authentic faith governs our lives.

I remember my mentor J. I. Packer telling us in a class that this type of situation is the crossroads of true Christian living. "The happy state," Dr. Packer said, "which we know only rarely, is the unself-

> *When we learn to truly delight in the welfare of others and rejoice in what God is doing in their lives, the potential for increased joy skyrockets.*

conscious state in which all our attention is being given to the people around us, to the situation outside us, and we're forgetting ourselves in the service of others. You see that to perfection in the life of Jesus."[6]

Rather than drink from the satisfying waters of selflessness, our culture has developed a dangerous appetite for the bitter drink of selfishness. I was asked to write an article on selflessness for a Christian magazine I highly respect. These people get it right far more often than not. After I submitted the article, I received an E-mail from the editor praising much of the article, then going on to make this request: "What we need now is for you to beef up the section on the rewards of selflessness."

I understand what the editor was trying to do—the topic could appear very negative—but it seemed to me almost comically ironic that our culture is saying, in a sense, "I'm willing to be less selfish, but if I do that, *what's in it for me?* Where's my reward?" Even in our selflessness, we are prone to adopt a selfish attitude!

The great irony, of course, is that the ancients do testify to the

> *Rather than drink from the satisfying waters of selflessness, our culture has developed the a dangerous appetite for the bitter drink of selfishness.*

many rewards of selflessness, making my editor's request not entirely inappropriate. But when you revisit Paul's astonishing statement in Romans 9:3, where he says he would choose damnation for the sake of others, you realize that "reward" as motivation to become less selfish can take us only so far; it will never usher us into the joyful self-abandonment experienced by Jesus, Paul, Augustine, and C. S. Lewis.

Keep in mind, this selflessness isn't reserved solely for mature Christians. Paul urges all of us to adopt it. "Do nothing out of selfish ambition or vain conceit," he tells the Philippians, "but in humility consider others better than yourselves. *Each of you* should look not only to your own interests, but also to the interests of others" (Philippians 2:3–4, emphasis added).

Spiritual health—in Paul's mind, at least—is marked by a vibrant, others-centered compassion and concern. Far from simply absorbing blessings, we are called to lavish God's love on others.

Self-Centered Ministry

The joy of selflessness also affects *how* we minister. One day a Christian man invited me to lunch. After a short chat, he asked me how I handle temptations on the road. I had just written a magazine article on this very subject and was full of answers, anecdotes, and advice. For over forty-five minutes, I "blessed" him with my astounding wisdom, insight, and practical strategies.

I came home from that lunch quite exhausted—but also frustrated, feeling certain that I hadn't been any help to him at all. The next morning, as I prayed about what had happened during this lunch encounter, I realized why I had been unhelpful and why I was feeling frustrated. This brother's question, "How do you handle temptation on the road, Gary?" wasn't the question he really wanted answered. Certainly, that was the question he verbalized, but it wasn't truly what he wanted to know. The question burning in his soul was, rather, "Gary, how can I handle temptation on the road?"

Because he had framed the question with me as the subject, I went down the wrong trail. I was full of myself, and I gave him myself, but what he really needed was to encounter God.

In order to answer my friend's real question, I needed to listen before I spoke. I should have asked him questions rather than spewed out my answers. I should have sought the genesis of *his* temptations rather than assume they were the same as mine. And I should have helped him find *his* exodus rather than proudly display my own.

I rose from prayer, eager to see God destroy this cursed self-obsession. It is so easy to fall into such a focus—after all, my friend had invited me to do so—but so harmful. If I am to help people and lead a contemplative, God-directed life, the first thing I must do is die to myself. If I had relied on God during that lunch meeting, carefully and prayerfully seeking what the Spirit would do during our hour and a half together, God would have led us to the real issues in this man's life. Instead, I was too eager to come up with principles and answers that were limited to my own experience, and not necessarily what this man needed to hear.

This is precisely why I long to mature in the faith. I don't fear that somehow my immaturity will keep me out of heaven. My destiny is secure in the finished, completed work of Jesus Christ. What my immaturity does more than anything is hinder God's work through me. Yes, he can work quite well in spite of my failings; but his ministry through me will become far more effective as I leave my old selfish habits and ways of relating behind. The immature might be on their way to heaven, but they rarely see deeply changed lives.

> *If I am to help people and lead a contemplative, God-directed life, the first thing I must do is die to myself.*

The danger is that we can become self-serving even in our service! Some might want to serve so that they can be admired and praised and feel wanted and needed. Precisely to counter this tendency, Paul stressed to the Corinthians that we should desire those spiritual gifts that *build up the church* and *edify others* (see 1 Corinthians 14:12). Even in the way God uses us, our motivation should be others-oriented, focused on the needs of our local Christian community.

Selflessness is far more a liberating truth than it is just another religious obligation, however. Going back through my journal one time, an entry caught my eye. I was feeling a bit overwhelmed and anxious about all that I had to do in the coming months, and I found solace in something I had written many months before: *God hasn't lost courage. God isn't wavering on endurance. God doesn't fear another day, another test, and God is standing behind me. He is making available for me all that he is. By grace, through faith, I have nothing to fear, no reason to feel defeated.*

The words struck me as though someone else had written them. Clearly, this had come from prayer, and I had forgotten all about it, but just to be reminded of its truth felt like a late-afternoon explosion of sunlight into an otherwise dreary day. It was a spiritual bath, a refreshing liberation, when I remembered that ministry in its purest form is radically God-dependent and God-empowered. I was reminded of David's words, "I do not trust in my bow, my sword does not bring me victory; but you give us victory over our enemies, you put our adversaries to shame. In God we make our boast all day long" (Psalm 44:6–8).

> *Selflessness is far more a liberating truth than it is just another religious obligation.*

Paul had this same mind-set when he wrote to the Corinthians, "But by the grace of God I am what I am, and his grace to me was not without effect. No, I worked harder than all of them—yet not I, but the grace of God that was with me" (1 Corinthians 15:10). You have this marvelous mix of Paul paddling furiously while he is carried down the river by God's great current. This is a sentiment Peter shared as well: "If anyone serves, he should do it with the strength God provides, so that in all things God may be praised through Jesus Christ" (1 Peter 4:11).

David, Paul, and Peter—three central characters in the Bible—and all three of them testified to learning the secret of working with God's strength, of leaning into the wind of God's Spirit and letting that Spirit enable them to do what they could never do on their own. The authentic faith of selflessness, then, focuses our minds and hearts on serving God by serving others. It affects not only where we minister and what we celebrate but also *how* we minister and *whose strength* we are dependent on.

Living beyond Your Self

How do we put all this into practice?

First, we must ask ourselves, How are we adopting Christ's passion for his body, the church? You may be doing everything seemingly right individually, but what is your role in Christ's community? God has blessed you. Wonderful! Now how are you going to use that blessing to bless and build up others?

Second, we must ask ourselves, How are we looking after others in our vocational and social lives? I told Orel Hershiser's story because most of us will not be called to make the kind of great sacrifice that Augustine made. Our selflessness will be played out on a much smaller scale, as Orel's was. Perhaps you'll find yourself coming into work early, at 7:30 a.m., to catch up on addressing 1,500 envelopes

> *The authentic faith of selflessness focuses our minds and hearts on serving God by serving others.*

for invitations to a seminar that your group is sponsoring. You're hoping to have it done by 9:00, but just as you're getting up to speed, you notice one of the new secretaries over in the corner cubicle, someone who was hired just two weeks ago. She's bent over her typewriter, clutching a tissue to her face. Her shoulders are shaking, *but you're really busy.* What will you do?

Wherever we go—whether it's the golf course, a church conference room, a restaurant, or the local mall—we have the opportunity to open up our eyes to what is happening to others around us, to think thoughts bigger than those that concern only us, and to be used by God—if only just by *noticing* others—by caring, in large ways and small, and by getting involved.

Finally, we observed that selflessness means "God-dependence." Let's say your pastor and several trusted friends notice a gift you haven't been using—or perhaps they present an opportunity for service that sounds inviting and that fits right in with what you believe God has called you to do—but you're bothered with the nagging question, "Am I qualified to do that?" Christians who let their weaknesses and inadequacies hold them back are just as self-focused as are believers who use their strengths to build self-glorifying kingdoms. When will we learn that it's not about us? God is not impressed by our gifts, nor is he frightened by our inadequacies.

God-dependence also means that we will slow down in the midst of our ministry, making way for God's still, small voice, his gentle whisper, to guide us. The next time you're listening to someone pour out their heart or voice a complaint or ask for your advice, what well will you draw from? Whose shoulder will you lean on? As we engage ourselves on the front lines of ministry, let's check our hurry at the door, be fully present in the moment, and invite God to take the lead.

Authentic Faith

> *Christians who let their weaknesses and inadequacies hold them back are just as self-focused as are believers who use their strengths to build self-glorifying kingdoms.*

There's an oft-told story about a remarkable relationship forged during the terrible field battles of World War I. I like to read a lot of military history, and as best I can tell, the story is true.

World War I was a particularly bad war to be a part of, not that there is such a thing as a "good" war, I suppose; but if you were a grunt during World War I, you were likely to face the even more inhumane trauma of trench warfare. Trench warfare was characterized by an abundance of downtime, mixed in with moments of sheer, unadulterated terror.

During the downtime, two American soldiers bonded tightly as they talked about their families, what they wanted to do when the war was over, and even, on occasion, how they dealt with the fear of living so close to so many men whose only mission in life was to end theirs.

One night the order was given for the soldiers to leave their trench and attack the enemy. The fighting was fierce and desperate, and the two friends got separated. After a long and arduous battle, the call went out to retreat back to the safety of the trench. When the one soldier returned, he began asking about his buddy, finally discovering that his friend was still out there, wounded and bleeding. Without even considering the danger, he announced that he was going back to get his friend.

"Absolutely not," the commanding officer replied. "It's suicidal to go back out there, and it's not worth the risk. I've already lost more men than I can afford to lose."

The soldier waited until the officer's head was turned, then jumped out of the relative safety of the trench and crawled toward his wounded buddy. Immediately, he was forced to pay the price—the mind-splitting reverberations of the shelling, the smoke hacking at his throat and making him cough, and the bullets flying overhead, which had the added, gruesome effect of keeping his face smashed into the blood-and-gore-infested ground.

Still, he crawled on until he reached his friend, shared a few words, and then began pulling him back toward the trench. Somewhere between the time he reached his buddy and the time they both made it back to the trench, the wounded friend died. With great sorrow, the friend pulled a precious corpse into the trench.

"So, was it worth it?" the officer barked, angry that his order had been disobeyed.

"Absolutely," the friend replied. "My buddy's final words made it all worthwhile."

"What could he have possibly said that made it worth risking your life to hear?" the officer shouted.

"When I reached him, he saw my face and said, 'I knew you'd come.'"

In a culture that celebrates the self, that calls us to be true to ourselves, there is a prophetic power released when people act with selflessness, when they learn to put others first and even to sacrifice themselves on another's behalf.

> *"When I reached him, he saw my face and said, 'I knew you'd come.'"*

1. See Romans 12:1–13; 1 John 3:16–20.

2. Augustine, "Enchiridion," chap.31, in *St. Augustine: On the Holy Trinity, Doctrinal Treatises, Moral Treatises,* vol.3, *A Select Library of the Nicene and Post-Nicene Fathers of the Christian Church,* ed. Philip Schaff (1887; reprint, Grand Rapids: Eerdmans, 1998), 248, emphasis added.

3. Augustine, *The City of God,* bk. 10, chap.6, trans. Henry Bettenson (New York: Penguin Books, 1972), 380.

4. Cited in George B. Sayer, *Jack: C. S. Lewis and His Times* (San Francisco: Harper San Francisco, 1988), 170–71.

5. Sayer, *Jack: C. S. Lewis and His Times,* 161.

6. J. I. Packer, "Sin," *Systematic Theology B,* Tape Series 2645 (Vancouver, B.C.: Regent College, 1996).

Acknowledgements

Jim Cymbala, *The Life God Blesses*, 2001, Zondervan, Grand Rapids, Michigan. All rights reserved.

John Ortberg, *The Life You've Always Wanted*, 1997, 2002, Zondervan, Grand Rapids, Michigan All rights reserved.

Gary L. Thomas, *Authentic Faith*, 2002, Zondervan, Grand Rapids, Michigan. All rights reserved.

Rick Warren, *The Purpose Driven Life*, 2002, Zondervan, Grand Rapids, Michigan. All rights reserved.

Michael Yaconelli, *Messy Spirituality*, 2002, Zondervan, Grand Rapids, Michigan. All rights reserved.

ACTION STEPS

_____

_____

_____

_____

_____

_____

_____

_____

_____

_____

_____

_____

_____

_____

_____

_____

_____

ACTION STEPS

_____

_____

_____

_____

_____

_____

_____

_____

_____

_____

_____

_____

_____

_____

_____

_____

Family
CHRISTIAN STORES

Coupon Valid
5/1-6/30/03

MAKE YOUR OWN SALE!

SAVE **$5** | on your purchase of **$35⁰⁰** or more

SAVE **$10** | on your purchase of **$60⁰⁰** or more

SAVE **$15** | on your purchase of **$85⁰⁰** or more

Family
CHRISTIAN STORES

Coupon Valid
7/1-8/31/03

MAKE YOUR OWN SALE!

SAVE **$5** | on your purchase of **$35⁰⁰** or more

SAVE **$10** | on your purchase of **$60⁰⁰** or more

SAVE **$15** | on your purchase of **$85⁰⁰** or more

Helping to Strengthen Hearts, Minds & Souls

943699

Sales associate key as FCS NON-FLYER COUPON ($)

Helping to Strengthen Hearts, Minds & Souls

943700

Sales associate key as FCS NON-FLYER COUPON ($)

FAMILY
CHRISTIAN STORES

Coupon Valid 9/1-10/31/03

MAKE YOUR OWN SALE!

SAVE **$5** | on your purchase of **$35**⁰⁰ or more

SAVE **$10** | on your purchase of **$60**⁰⁰ or more

SAVE **$15** | on your purchase of **$85**⁰⁰ or more

FAMILY
CHRISTIAN STORES

Coupon Valid 11/1-12/31/03

MAKE YOUR OWN SALE!

SAVE **$5** | on your purchase of **$35**⁰⁰ or more

SAVE **$10** | on your purchase of **$60**⁰⁰ or more

SAVE **$15** | on your purchase of **$85**⁰⁰ or more

CHRISTIAN STORES

Helping to Strengthen Hearts, Minds & Souls

943701

Sales associate key as FCS NON-FLYER COUPON ($)

CHRISTIAN STORES

Helping to Strengthen Hearts, Minds & Souls

943702

Sales associate key as FCS NON-FLYER COUPON ($)